COLLINS CONCISE GUIDE TO
THE UPLANDS
OF BRITAIN

COLLINS CONCISE GUIDE TO
THE UPLANDS OF BRITAIN

Michael Marriott

Willow Books
Collins
8 Grafton Street, London
1983

Willow Books
William Collins Sons & Co Ltd
London · Glasgow · Sydney
Auckland ·Toronto · Johannesburg

First published in Great Britain 1983

Marriott, Michael
Collins concise guide to the uplands of Britain.
1. Mountains – Great Britain – Guide-books
2. Great Britain – Description and travel – 1971
   – Guide-books
I. Title
914.1'04858 DA650

ISBN 0 00 218014 6

Designed and produced by
Quintet Publishing Limited, London
Editorial Director   Clare Howell
Editor   Hilary Dickinson
Art Editor   Christopher White
Design   Rose & Lamb Design
                          Partnership
Illustrations   Sue Rose
Cartographer   John Mitchell

Phototypeset by
Hugh Wilson Typesetting, Norwich

Illustrations originated by
East Anglian Engraving Ltd, Norwich

Printed and bound in Italy by L.E.G.O. Vicenza

Contents

Introduction

The *Collins Concise Guide to the Uplands of Britain* has been compiled primarily for the less experienced explorer, to enable him, or her, to assess the walking or climbing potential of every accessible upland area. It is designed as a practical reference, small enough to fit in a rucksack or the glove compartment of a car. The areas have been arranged by physical groupings under relevant descriptive headings which enables easy location, comparison, and selection. The guide covers high moors, hill ranges, and mountains, and also includes the downlands, sea-cliffs and heritage coasts, and all major offshore islands which contain high country or offer dramatic cliff-top walking.

The book is designed as a pathfinder and does not obviate the need for Ordnance Survey maps or detailed guide-books written expressly about given areas, long-distance paths, or climbing grounds. Its value is rather for those who are embarking perhaps for the first time on the pursuit of high country exploration. In any book of this size which is attempting to cover the whole of Britain, brevity is obviously vital. The limitations of space preclude more than a passing mention in some cases. However, each entry has been chosen with due care, and mere inclusion is significant. The reader is provided with all the clues to the discovery of the most exhilarating and beautiful upland areas from the south coast to the Shetlands.

The Essential Information panels are basically self-explanatory. The height figures give an idea of the effort likely to be expended: the greater the range of average height, the more strenuous the walk. Mileages are approximate and are measured as the crow flies. Suggested bases are towns or villages, where possible acknowledged as visitor centres, otherwise chosen for practical or scenic appeal, and preferably both.

The access routes listed provide the most convenient and direct entry points to an area. With a few exceptions the road numbers may be found on small-scale motoring maps, given that large-scale detailed versions will not always be available. The BR stations are as close to selected areas as possible, and are generally mainline stops. Local enquiries can sometimes produce more convenient halts. Youth hostels are included under their named headings, but for detailed addresses the relevant Association Handbook should be consulted.

Michael Marriott

Climbing

Rock-climbing is the art of ascending steep rock and has been called 'ballet in a vertical idiom'. While it is one of the several complementary skills of mountaineering, it is often practised for its own sake. It is an idiosyncratic game, its only rules being a loose code of generally accepted ethics, little understood by the layman. The climbing paragraphs of this book may need some qualification.

No attempt has been made to list all the climbing in Britain, or indeed the best of it, but rather a representative sample of what is available in the areas covered by the main text. Sometimes 'classic' or recommended climbs are suggested (marked *). The grade, length, and date of first ascent will give an idea of the 'style' of the climbing. Long and ancient low-grade routes may be broken and grassy but good fun in poor conditions. Short modern routes are often hard, mean, and very technical. Very short climbs may be 'top-roped' to give experience to novices, and so on. The rock type will also indicate much: for instance, limestone is typically vertical with small-cut holes, while gabbro is rarely steep but offers terrific friction.

Technical standards are often controversial. The basic 'grades' are: Difficult (D), Very Difficult (VD), Severe (S), Very Severe (VS), and Extreme (XS), with a sub-grading of Hard (e.g. HVD). Today's XS grade covers a greater range of difficulty than the sum of all the others. Novices will find the D and VD grades more suitable.

It is probably true to say that winter climbing is the most important form of the game in the Scottish Highlands. There are 544 Scottish mountains above 3000 feet, and for six months each year they may be plastered in snow and ice. Conditions and grades may change from day to day, but easy summer rock climbs may become serious mountaineering expeditions, and good winter routes may be found on some mountains with no crags at all. Where applicable, the winter importance of Scottish locations is indicated.

Mountaineering has a huge literature and most climbing areas are exhaustively described in special guide-books. Take advice from your local mountain/outdoor shop or climbing club. Alternatively, contact the British Mountaineering Council (B.M.C.), or go on a residential course. The distances quoted are map distances, and no guarantees can be given about access and rights of way.

John Cleare

Equipment

In perfect weather it is obviously possible to walk many of the British hills in city clothes – but not in comfort or even in safety. The sterner the landscape, the more serious the potential weather, and the more essential the appropriate clothing and equipment. In winter the most gentle hills can become killers, while those who venture, even in summer, on our moorlands and mountains expecting settled weather, do so at their peril. Summer or winter the threat of exposure or hypothermia is a potentially lethal hazard for the ill-equipped. Some of the basic equipment for hill-walking is shown below, together with specialist equipment for rock-climbing.

The new lightweight walking boots made of fabric and leather are excellent in most conditions. A special sole with cleats and studs prevents clogging.

Specialist lightweight rock-climbing slippers made of suede or fabric with a smooth rubber sole give excellent friction properties for harder technical climbs.

Mountain walking boots should be tough but flexible. A patterned Vibram sole is essential.

Gaiters, made of canvas or nylon, help to prevent wet feet and are useful when negotiating bogs and mud.

Clothing should provide warmth and protection but should be light in weight and comfortable so that movement is not restricted. Waterproofs should also be windproof, with welded seams, storm cuffs and collar, hood, and protected zip; Derby tweed breeches are the best choice (above). A duvet jacket with a special fibre filling gives maximum insulation without extra weight (right).

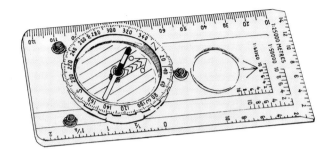

A compass is a vital piece of equipment – but you must know how to use it. The Silva orienteering compass is a good choice.

Rucksacks should be chosen with care to ensure a perfect fit. The integral frame should be contoured to the back for maximum comfort and for stability when scrambling or climbing. The larger types have a padded hip belt and shoulder straps.

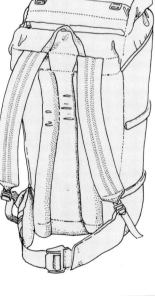

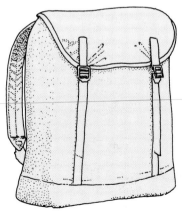

A small day sack is ideal for carrying the spare clothing, food, and map that will be needed on a short expedition.

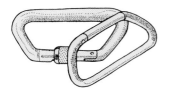

Several alloy snap-link karabiners should be carried, including one with a screw-gate.

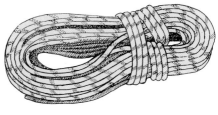

A 150-foot length of 11 mm kernmantle rope is usually carried. Choose a reputable brand with a guarantee of test safety.

A special climbing helmet is essential, as much to guard against falling stones as against the climber himself falling.

An ice axe should be carried if there is snow on the hills. Its most important function is self-arrest on steep slopes; it should just be long enough to use as a walking-stick.

Crampons may be vital for safety, particularly in winter conditions on Scottish mountains.

Practical Information

The Country Code

Walkers should abide by the Country Code. Its rules are few and simple, and by observing them rigidly we can all help to preserve the countryside and an atmosphere of trust between town and country dwellers.

Guard against all risk of fire

Fasten all gates

Keep dogs under control

Keep to rights of way across farmland

Avoid damaging fences, hedges, and walls

Leave no litter

Safeguard water supplies

Protect wildlife, plants, and trees

Go carefully on country roads

Respect the life of the countryside

The Walker and the Law

● There are over 100 000 miles of public footpaths in Britain which are legally accessible to the walker. If the path is also a bridleway, you may ride a horse or cycle along it.

● You are only entitled to walk on the footpath or bridleway, not on adjacent land. Even in remote country you do not have the right to camp, light fires, pick flowers, or leave rubbish. This applies to fells and moorland, and is especially important in farmland and forests.

● Close all farm gates and keep dogs under control.

● If a marked path passes through a field of corn you are entitled to follow it, but make sure you do as little damage as possible.

● Take adequate care if a footpath crosses land grazed by bulls. Keep away from the animals and do not startle them by sudden noises or movements.

Safety in the Hills

● Do not walk alone until you are sufficiently experienced and confident. Know your own limitations – and adhere to them.

● Do not go into new terrain unprepared. Plan each expedition adequately with map and compass. Find out the best access and escape routes.

● It is advisable to walk in company. Three is a good number: if an emergency arises, one person can go for help while the other stays with the injured person.

● Err on the side of caution when planning a walk, in terms of both distance and weather conditions. Remember that the weather can change rapidly at high altitudes.

● Always leave word of your destination and intended route before setting out into the hills. If you cannot inform someone at your base, then even a note attached to the windscreen of your car will do.

● Make sure you carry emergency survival gear: extra warm clothing, quick-energy foods (e.g. chocolate), means of making a hot drink, a first-aid kit, whistle, and torch.

● Memorize the recognized distress signal: six long flashes or six long whistle blasts in quick succession, followed by a pause of one minute.

● If you get into a difficult situation, the thing is not to panic. Stop, think, then take appropriate action. Above all, do not rush down the mountain – this could get you into even more trouble. Stay put, find shelter if you can, keep warm, and wait for help to come.

Key to maps

△	Youth hostels
□	Hotels or ancient sites
▲	Heights in feet
▲▲	Major climbing centres
ᴧᴛᴛ	Sea-cliffs

High Moors

The high moors of these islands exert a strong attraction for those who develop a relish for hard walking. Bog-trotting, as it is both affectionately and aptly known by enthusiasts (especially in northern England), demands reserves of strength, navigational expertise, and a certain disregard of personal comfort.

Most moorland traverses involve rough going, usually interspersed with stretches of wet and boggy terrain, and pockets of civilization are often few and far between. By their very nature the moors are lonely and stern, sometimes bleak and even verging on hostile. But it is precisely this which provides the challenge so many walkers seem to want. Endurance, self-reliance, and a strong competitive streak are the qualities of good bog-trotters, who find deep pleasure in taking on the wind-swept world of the moors, where the skyline is broken only by occasional rock outcrops.

Moorland distance-walking, while quite popular with all

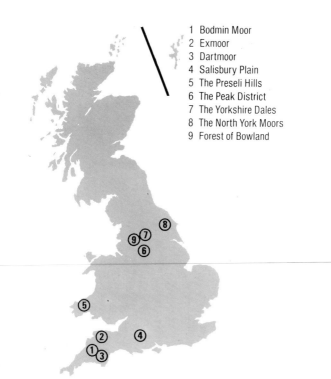

1 Bodmin Moor
2 Exmoor
3 Dartmoor
4 Salisbury Plain
5 The Preseli Hills
6 The Peak District
7 The Yorkshire Dales
8 The North York Moors
9 Forest of Bowland

walkers, is primarily the pursuit of those in the 40 to 60 age group; statistically those walkers with the most highly developed reserves of sustainable stamina which the pursuit requires. Newcomers should keep to the outer, usually less stern, edges of the moorland tracts; in these instructive training grounds the novice can sample the subtle yet seductive beauty of Britain's high moors before plunging into real wilderness. The first complete crossing of any of Britain's recognized moors is an achievement to instil lasting personal satisfaction in any walker, together with an exhilarating sense of physical and mental challenge.

Practical Points

● Proficiency with map and compass is essential as visibility is often restricted, despite the wide open spaces. The ability to navigate correctly inspires confidence and conserves strength.

● When embarking on a trek over a three-day week-end, keep the mileage on the second day modest, especially if you are out of training. Moorland walking saps stamina – notably after heavy rain – and many walkers give up at the middle of day two. By day three, second wind is usually regained.

● Time and distance sometimes become surprisingly protracted. Avoid over-optimism and always carry extra supplies like quick-energy food and spare clothing in case of emergency.

● Despite good waterproofs and high-quality boots, you will invariably be wet by the end of a day of moorland walking, either from rain or simple physical exertion. Dry clothing and socks (protected in plastic bags in your pack) work wonders for morale and soon revive the spirits. Peat puddles have a high acidic content so be sure to dowse boots with fresh water to prevent the leather from rotting.

● Wind usually varies only from irritating to threatening on the high moors. Put on waterproofs to offset chill; wear sun-glasses against the worst of peat dust which is often stirred up in dry, windy conditions.

● Plan every expedition with military precision before setting out, particularly if you are inexperienced or at less than peak physical condition. Study the relevant OS maps beforehand, pinpointing escape routes and havens. Remember the trusted formula which decrees one hour for every three miles on the map, plus one hour more for every 2000 feet of altitude.

Bodmin Moor

Essential Information

Height: Average between 800 and 1000 ft; max. Brown Willy (1377 ft)
Area: South-east to north-west 15 miles; south-west to north-east 12 miles
Distances from main towns:
Launceston 7 miles; Liskeard 4 miles; Bodmin 2 miles
Suggested bases: Bodmin, Camelford, St Breward
Access routes: Via A30 between Launceston and Bodmin
BR stations: Liskeard, Bodmin Road
Youth hostels: Boscastle Harbour, Tintagel
OS map: 201

A principal outcrop of Cornish granite underlies the plateau of Bodmin Moor, shot through with tin and copper veins. While rainfall is high (up to 80 inches a year), the climate is peculiarly Cornish as snow is rare and winters are more temperate than anywhere else in Britain. This does not mean that Bodmin Moor can be treated lightly, even in high summer. Mists are frequent, intense, and often very cold.

It is a drab landscape of rough grass with wide stretches of bog and marsh, but on the borders of the moor wooded valleys offer a gentler aspect. Studded with prehistoric remains, the moor is one of Britain's most primitive upland regions, with a fascination best appreciated by the walker.

Brown Willy and Rough Tor

The main area of high ground rises in the northern part of the moor and contains two of the highest peaks in the county: Brown Willy (1377 feet) and Rough Tor (1311 feet). A variety of routes lead to Brown Willy, a favoured ascent being via the footpath which starts at Codda Farm, ¾ mile north of Bolventnor. Although often

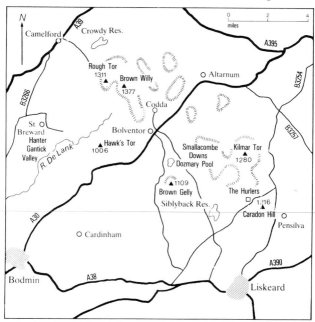

Cheesewring: a granite tor near Minions.

shrouded in mist, the summit offers spectacular views over the surrounding country in good weather.

Rough Tor, Bodmin's second highest peak, can be reached from the north via a minor road south-east from Camelford which ends some 3 miles from the Tor; a well-trodden track leads from the end of the road to the summit. Two miles south-west of Rough Tor stands King Arthur's Hall, an ancient enclosure lined with granite slabs, said to have been built some 4000 years ago.

The western moor

In the western part of the moor lie yet more spectacular places worthy of exploration. The Hanter Gantick Valley, a craggy gorge with a rushing stream, extends to the east of the granite quarries on the De Lank river. Some 3 miles north is Hannon Valley, another beauty spot, particularly near the valley known as the Devil's Jump.

The central moor

From Bolventnor at the heart of the moor a minor road runs to Liskeard, at the southern edge. A number of paths lead from the road, notably to the vast and bleak expanse of Dozmary Pool into which King Arthur is reputed to have cast his sword Excalibur. Further tracks run across Smallacombe Downs, a remote area of wild terrain.

The south-east

In the south-east loom Kilmar Tor (1280 feet), above Twelve Men's Moor, and Stowe's Hill. Some 4 miles north of Liskeard near Minions stand The Hurlers, a large group of prehistoric stones. This is just one of several strange groups scattered over the moor; perhaps the most evocative is Stripple Stones, on the southern slopes of Hawk's Tor Downs.

Climbing Information

Good **granite** in moorland settings.
● **Cheesewring Quarry** (258 724) near Minions 5 m. N. of Liskeard. Over 40 climbs up to 150 ft in impressive amphitheatre, longer ones hard and serious but also shorter easier climbs and boulder problems.
* 'Eye-full Tower': 120 ft. HVS (1967) **Cheesewring** near by, spectacular 25-ft overhanging tor. XS or combined tactics.
● **Devil's Jump** (103 800): twin tors in pleasant valley setting 2 m. SW. of Camelford.
* 'SE Climb': 75 ft. VD (1921); and other climbs
Several other hill-top tors give boulder problems up to 25 ft e.g. **Rough Tor** (145 807) and **Hawk's Tor** (254 764).
● **Roche Rock** (992 597) 6 m. SW. of Bodmin, strictly speaking on St Austell Moor. Enjoyable un-serious problems up to 60 ft on tor crowned by ruined chapel.

Exmoor

Essential Information

Height: Average between 1000 and 1400 ft; max. Dunkery Beacon (1705 ft)

Area: North–south 12 miles; east–west 20 miles

Distances from main towns: Minehead 2 miles; Ilfracombe 4 miles; Barnstaple 7 miles

Suggested bases: Lynton, Dulverton, Dunster

Access routes: A39 (north) between Minehead and Blackmoor Gate; B3224 and B3358 (central); A361 (south) from South Molton

BR stations: Minehead, Barnstaple

Youth hostels: Lynton, Minehead, Exford

OS maps: 180, 181

Geologically Exmoor is largely Devonian sandstone, some 265 square miles more accurately known as Exmoor Forest, now protected as one of Britain's smallest National Parks. Though crossed by numerous roads there are still appreciable wild areas where red deer and the native Exmoor ponies roam. Exmoor offers strongly contrasting scenery: desolate plateaux of bracken and heather, steep and richly wooded combes, and magnificent coastline. Rainfall is heavy, and the northern part of the area is cut by numerous streams that rush down from the moorland heights. Some of the best pedestrian routes follow these steep water-courses.

Dunkery Beacon

Dunkery Beacon, at 1705 feet the highest point on Exmoor, commands the central heights on Dunkery Hill, and rewards the walker with exhilarating views westwards towards the coast and northwards to the Welsh mountains. The way-marked route from Wheddon Cross on the A396 between

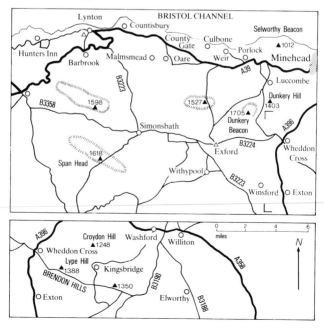

Steep moorland slopes richly clad in bracken inland of Lynmouth.

Dunster and Dulverton is a wind-swept and at times stern trudge. There is another approach from Luccombe, by a path which runs on the seaward side of the hill.

To the east lie the Brendon Hills, offering gentler terrain of hedged fields and stone farmsteads. There are well-marked footpaths into the Brendon area from the villages which lie along the A396 Exebridge to Minehead road.

The eastern part of Exmoor inland from the A39 is properly known as Lorna Doone country. From the village of Oare, near County Gate, there is a pleasant 5-mile circular walk via Lorna Doone Farm at Malmsmead and on to the Blackmore Memorial and Badgworthy Water.

The Barle Valley

Numerous walks run through the Barle Valley in the southern part of the moor below Exford: to Withypool Hill (1306 feet), its summit dominated by a prehistoric barrow and stone circle, and over Withypool Common. One notable 4-mile route runs from Withypool to Tarr Steps, which has one of the most ancient and celebrated clapper bridges in the country, following the banks of the River Barle for almost all of its length.

The Exmoor coast

Exmoor's coast offers a wealth of exhilarating walks; one particularly fine stretch extends from Minehead to the western boundary of the National Park. This is part of the South-West Peninsula long-distance path and gives nearly 30 miles of exhilarating walking along majestic wooded cliffs, taking in such high spots as Porlock Weir, Culbone (which boasts England's smallest church), Countisbury, the Valley of the Rocks, and Hunter's Inn.

There is further fine walking over the headland above Lynmouth. A footpath route starts near the A39 between Barbrook and Lynton, running up and over the Cleave and then dropping down to Watersmeet, giving wide views over deep wooded valleys and out to sea.

19

Dartmoor

Essential Information

Height: Average between 1500 and 1900 ft; max. High Willhays (2038 ft)
Area: North–south 25 miles; east–west 17 miles
Distances from main towns: Exeter 8 miles; Plymouth 6 miles; Torquay 12 miles
Suggested bases: Okehampton, Tavistock, Ashburton
Access routes: Via A30 (north); A38 (south); B3212 (central)
BR stations: Okehampton, Buckfastleigh
Youth hostels: Bellever, Gidleigh, Steps Bridge
OS maps: 191, 201, 202

The 365 square miles of the Dartmoor National Park comprise one of the last untamed stretches of country in southern England. It is a landscape of contrast: a vast central granite plateau topped with massive tors that rise above bleak marshes, and lush river valleys which run down from the high moorland. The upland bogs can be a hazard to the walker, particularly when the swirling mists descend.

With some 460 miles of public rights of way (footpath and bridlepath) and nearly 99 000 acres of common land, Dartmoor offers a wealth of possibilities for the walker. While car-borne visitors will see only those parts of the moor which lie immediately adjacent to the roads, and the well-known scenic spots, the walker can escape the crowds with very little effort. It is possible to walk virtually anywhere, on the open moor and in the newtakes, the uncultivated walled enclosures.

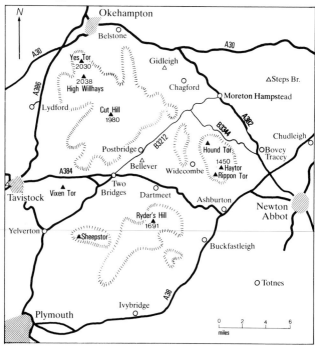

Haytor 'Low Man' (1450 feet).

The central moor

This area is probably the most popular with walkers. It is easily accessible by car as the two main roads over the moor, the B3212 and B3357, cross at Two Bridges. From Two Bridges extend miles of open country. Dartmeet, between Two Bridges and Ashburton, is popular, but it is easy to find seclusion by following the path by the River West Dart.

Postbridge, north of Two Bridges on the B3212, is the best base; a track from the car park leads into the northern area of the moor. Numerous paths start at Postbridge, including a footpath to the peat-covered summit of Cut Hill (1980 feet), far from any road.

Footpaths and back lanes lead from Widecombe in the Moor to Haytor Rocks (1450 feet) and the Bovey Valley. From here the more experienced walker can plan a day's exploration of the eastern summits such as Saddle Tor and Rippon Tor, while the novice can join one of the guided walks which start from the car park at the foot of the Rocks.

The northern moor

The most dramatic heights lie in the north-eastern corner of the moor, particularly in the area south of Okehampton.

From Okehampton there is easy access by path to Yes Tor (2030 feet) and High Willhays (2038 feet), the highest peak on Dartmoor. Another path runs from the centre of Okehampton through the wooded valley of the East Okement river to Belstone and Belstone Skaigh, returning to Okehampton along back lanes and footpaths.

Numerous paths radiate from Chagford in the Teign Valley, one eastwards to Steps Bridge via Fingle Bridge, another along the ancient Mariners' Way between the hamlet of Throwleigh and Widecombe; both offer some 10 miles of way-marked walking through splendid scenery.

Climbing Information

Most climbing is on the numerous hill-top tors, excellent coarse **granite**, typically steep and bulging.
● **Haytor** and **Low Man** (758 771): twin tors at 1450 ft in open moorland 7 m. NW. of Newton Abbot, popular tourist venue. Some 40 climbs of all kinds (cracks, chimneys, walls, slabs), from D to XS and up to 150 ft.
* 'Raven Gully': 105 ft. S (1949)
* 'Aviation': 130 ft. XS (1961)
● Other important tors: **Sheep's Tor** (567 682), **Vixen Tor** (543 743), **Hound Tor** (743 790), **Bonehill Rocks** (732 755).
● **Dewerstone** (538 638): several impressive buttresses rise from sheltered woodland of R. Plym gorge 8 m. N. of Plymouth. Over 50 climbs up to 195 ft typically vertical and serious at VS or harder, but some easier climbs.
* 'Colonel's Arete': 130 ft. VD (1948)
* 'Central Groove': 180 ft. VS (1949)
● **Chudleigh Rocks** (864 788): sound and steep Devonian **limestone** 4 m. N. of Newton Abbot in attractive woodland situation. More than 100 climbs (all grades), often on rock faces.
* 'Wogs': 120 ft. VD (1923)
* 'The Spider': 130 ft. HVS (1964)

Salisbury Plain

Essential Information

Height: Average between 500 and 700 ft; max. 945 ft north-west of Mere and White Sheet Hill

Area: North–south 12 miles; east–west 22 miles

Distances from main towns: Salisbury 5 miles; Devizes 3 miles; Andover 8 miles

Suggested bases: Salisbury, Devizes

Access routes: A342 (north) between Devizes and Andover; A303 (central) between Andover and Mere; A30 (south), Salisbury vicinity

BR stations: Salisbury, Andover, Pewsey

Youth hostel: Salisbury

OS map: 184

Salisbury Plain is a massive chalk upland that extends across some two-thirds of Wiltshire, rising in many places into steep and quite dramatic escarpments. It is extraordinarily rich in prehistoric relics and has for long been a base for the British Army who though they have scarred the land have also, paradoxically, preserved it against over-development. While Salisbury Plain may not be a moor in the sense of Dartmoor, it is still sufficiently akin to one, so far as the leisure walker is concerned, to qualify under that heading.

The rolling uplands of the plain extend to the north, east, and west. To the south the terrain slopes down into gentle, and lovely, valleys: the Wylye Valley with its straggle of villages, and the Woodford Valley below the shoulder of Amesbury Down, where the River Avon traces its course south.

Downland routes

The neolithic Great Ridgeway Iron Age track which runs

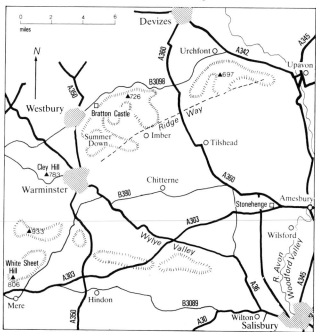

Silbury Hill, seen from the south-east.

south-west across the Plain, skirting Warminster, is just one of several prehistoric routes which are now largely obliterated. There are, though, pockets of old Wessex where the walker may tread in ancient footsteps. The Imber Perimeter Path is one, a circuitous route around a deserted village now used as an Army training ground. It is way-marked just north-east of Warminster, on Summer Down, and is well defined. The village itself is derelict, the small church fenced off to complete an evocative, if somewhat desolate, scene.

The village of Urchfont, south-east of Devizes, is another gateway to the historic landscape of Salisbury Plain. There are two main choices of route: across a scarp-edge stretch of the Ridgeway to the west, or over Wexcombe Down to the east.

At the far western end of the Plain, Harrow Way, one of Britain's most ancient trackways (once linking Dover with Axmouth in Devon), runs across White Sheet Hill above Mere. Close to the Dorset border, this is a fine downland path which climbs from an attractive and historic village to an imposing Iron Age hill-fort. North-west of here, above Warminster, lie the Westbury White Horse and the massive earthworks of Bratton Castle. At Cleyhill, about 3 miles west of the town, there are splendid views over the surrounding area from the hill-fort on its 800-foot vantage point.

At the heart of the Plain stands Stonehenge, the most famous, and most dramatic, of all stone circles. Despite the crush of visitors, the walker who chooses both time and season with care can take a thrilling approach route, north-west from the hamlet of Wilsford, on the banks of the Avon, some 2 miles south-west of Amesbury. There is more mystery – and one of the higher landmarks – at the man-made Silbury Hill at the eastern end of the Plain, near North Tidworth.

23

The Preseli Hills

Essential Information

Height: Average between 950 and 1100 ft; max. Preseli Top (1760 ft)

Area: North–south 6 miles; east–west 15 miles

Distances from main towns: Fishguard 3 miles; Cardigan 8 miles; Haverfordwest 9 miles

Suggested bases: Fishguard, Newport

Access routes: A478 (east) between Cardigan and Narberth; B4313 and B4329 (central); A487 and A40 (west), Fishguard vicinity

BR station: Fishguard

OS maps: 145, 158

The Preseli Hills, approached from Fishguard.

The Preseli Hills, Mynydd Preseli, may be hills in name, but in fact this curious and fascinating upland area in the north of Pembrokeshire is really a moorland tract of undulating summit peaks linked by an ancient ridgeway, known as the Roman Road, Ffordd Ffleming. The smooth but steep plateau rises from Crymych south of Cardigan and stretches west, giving spectacular views over the peninsula. The highest point is Preseli Top, Foelcwmcerwyn (1760 feet). The hills are of ancient origin,

principally of the Ordovician era, overlaid with igneous rocks, formed some 500 million years ago.

Much of north Pembrokeshire is low and covered in peat and scenically rather dull. The exception is the Preseli Hills, carpetted with heather and gorse, with contours more reminiscent of Worcestershire than west Wales. To find the best of the area, take either the B4313 or B4329 roads, which run up over the hills.

In prehistoric times these heights played an important part, both religious and secular. It was from Carnmenyn in the hills that the inner bluestones used to build Stonehenge were quarried and transported to Salisbury Plain, 150 miles away. The ridgeway was part of an ancient route linking Salisbury Plain with Whitesand Bay where trading boats set sail for Ireland. The numerous relics that lie scattered on the hills – burial mounds, stone circles, defensive earthworks – bear witness to this past.

Preseli Top

The road from Cardigan to Haverfordwest crosses the heights via the Pass of Winds and at Talfarn-y-bwlch is joined by a minor road from Nevern. From here a track winds upwards to the summit of Preseli Top. On a clear day the views extend from Snowdon to Cornwall and even westwards to the shores of Ireland. An alternative route begins at the Crymych Arms, on the Tenby road.

East of Preseli Top lies the isolated hamlet of Mynachlog-ddu, and near by a stone circle of fifteen boulders and pointer stones, almost resembling a miniature Stonehenge. From Maenclochog to the south-west, an old slate-quarrying centre, there are wide and splendid views.

Carn Igli

In the north-western corner of the district is one of the best-preserved prehistoric settlements in Wales, Carn Igli. Set on a rocky height at 1020 feet overlooking the village of Newport on the A487, it is reached via a lane behind the church.

The most beautiful approach road to the Preseli Hills leads from Fishguard south-east via the Gwaun Valley, passing through several charming hamlets, including Llanllawer; this area contains the largest of all Welsh prehistoric relics.

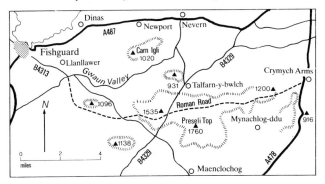

25

The Peak District

Essential Information

Height: Average between 1200 and 1600 ft; max. Kinder Scout (2088 ft)
Area: North–south 45 miles; east–west 20 miles
Distances from main towns: Manchester (centre) 10 miles; Sheffield (centre) 5 miles; Derby 14 miles
Suggested bases: Castleton, Edale, Ashbourne, Buxton, Bakewell
Access routes: A515 (south) between Ashbourne and Buxton; A57 (central) between Glossop and Sheffield; A625 between Chapel-en-le-Frith and Hathersage; A628/A6024 (north) between Stalybridge and Holmfirth
BR stations: Matlock, Buxton, Edale, Glossop, Penistone
Youth hostels: Ilam Hall, Hartington, Matlock Bath, Bakewell, Buxton, Castleton, Crowden-in-Longdendale, Edale (total of 26 within the National Park)
OS maps: 109, 110, 118, 119

The Peak District comprises some 540 square miles at the southern end of the Pennines, covering much of Derbyshire and taking in the edges of Staffordshire, Cheshire, Yorkshire, and a strip of Lancashire. The area can be divided into two distinct parts: the Dark Peak in the north, a rugged moorland plateau covered with peat and heather within precipitous gritstone outcrops and 'edges'; and the White Peak to the south, a limestone area of gentler terrain with lush dales and wooded river valleys.

Both Peaks offer excellent opportunities for walkers and climbers: bog-trotting over Kinder and Bleaklow in the Dark Peak, river-bank walking in the Dales, climbing the gritstone cliffs of Stanage Edge. In terms of climate, the Peak District has less rainfall than the hill and mountain ranges on the western coasts of Britain, in fact about half. The major hazard is the mist that can shroud the high ground and cut visibility with alarming rapidity.

The Dark Peak

The Dark Peak is considered by many to be the best walking area in central England. This rugged stretch of high country is rightly the preserve of experienced walkers, and the novice should not venture out alone, particularly in winter. It is dominated by the summits of Kinder Scout (2088 feet), Bleaklow Hill (2077 feet), and Black Hill (1908 feet). Hayfield is a convenient base from which to explore Kinder and Bleaklow, while Black Hill on the northern side of the Longdendale Valley can be approached from Holme.

There is yet more spectacular terrain to the east, around Hathersage in the Hope Valley, reached via the A57 from Glossop over Featherbed Top and via the Snake Pass. From Hathersage, School Lane climbs steeply to Stanage Edge, one of the most beautiful, and most popular, climbing centres in the Peak District; the 4-mile walk along the Edge gives truly magnificent views. For those who would walk rather than climb, there is a wide choice of moorland footpaths. The fine vantage points of Lose Hill (1563 feet) and Win Hill (1529 feet) rise to the north-west of Hathersage.

Kinder Scout

The vast peat wastes of Kinder Plateau cover an area some 5 miles long and 3 miles wide to the north of the Edale Valley. The full circuit of 22 miles provides an expedition of varied scenery, but it is a strenuous trek and only strong walkers will be able to complete it in a day. Kinder consists of a succession of tops, of which the highest is Kinder High (2088 feet); it can be difficult to locate the summit cairn, even from a distance of 25 yards, because of the uneven terrain.

The classic approach to the heights of Kinder starts at Edale village. The two most popular ascents are via Grindsbrook and Jacob's Ladder, west of Crowden Brook. The first is a stern trek involving some scrambling over boulder and scree on the edge of the plateau before it crosses the barren peat groughs to the Kinder river which is followed to Kinder Downfall. This 100-foot waterfall, a trickle in dry weather, is impressive in spate. The second route is easier and is often chosen in bad weather. The ascent of Kinder Scout forms the first stage of the Pennine Way.

The White Peak

The White Peak covers the area south of an imaginary line between Macclesfield and Sheffield down to Ashbourne. Although less rugged than the Dark Peak the terrain should not be treated lightly. Four river valleys – Derwent, Dove, Wye, and Manifold – cut through the area, offering an invigorating combination of scenery from limestone outcrops to fertile pastures. For the novice walker,

Kinder Scout. View east from White Brow towards Sandy Heys.

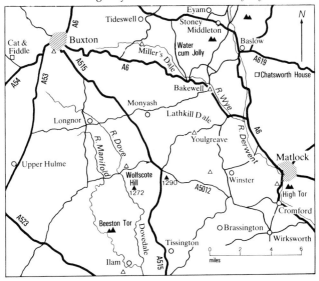

the Tissington and High Peak Trails provide an accessible introduction to typical Derbyshire landscape of dry-stone walls and steep-sided dales.

Each one of the many dales has much to offer. The Manifold Valley, 2 miles west of Ashbourne, is famous for the caves that riddle the scarp of Beeston Tor. Just 3 miles north-west of Buxton, the Goyt Valley in its moorland setting offers wooded paths, deep rocky ravines, and the expanse of the Errwood Reservoir; a scheme of restricted access to traffic ensures seclusion.

Dovedale

Possibly some of the most dramatic scenery is to be found in Dovedale, where towering limestone cliffs edge the beautiful, swift-flowing River Dove.

The narrow ravine has been carved out over the centuries by the action of the river, its sides weathered into strange and impressive shapes. The dramatic effect is increased by the tortuous course of the river; the walker who follows the path along the riverside is shown the dale in a series of breath-taking short stretches.

Fantastic spires and pinnacles outcrop along the whole length of the dale: Castle Rocks, the Twelve Apostles, Lovers' Leap, Lion Rock, Ilam Rock. The vast arches of rock at Reynard's Cave and the Dove Holes are more dramatic still. Dovedale has become a popular climbing centre bringing yet more visitors to the already crowded dale. The village of Ilam is a favoured starting-point for walking expeditions.

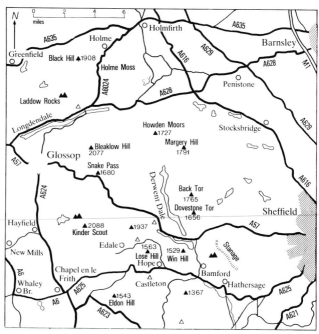

Climbing Information

The area contains arguably the most important 'non-mountain' rock-climbing in Britain. Hundreds of cliffs, mostly easily accessible, offer thousands of climbs of all kinds. Two very different kinds of crag:

1 Gritstone – **millstone grit** – a rough firm sandstone, extends as an escarpment along many moorland edges, outcrops on hill-sides as steep buttresses, or forms weird hill-top tors. Features such as walls, buttresses, chimneys, gullies, and towers abound, giving steep climbs (all standards), typically 40–50 ft, and strenuous with good cracks, excellent friction, and few incut holds. Climbs are often led but top-roping and soloing are popular. Protection is usually superb. Also much climbing in gritstone quarries, especially in the Bolton area.

The gritstone crag of Stanage Edge.

● **Stanage Edge** (225 865 to 246 832): some 4 m. of scarp contain over a mile of continuous cliff at 1500 ft altitude immediately N. of Hathersage village. Some 500 climbs (every grade) up to 80 ft.
* 'Right Unconquerable': 50 ft. HVS (1947)
* 'Goliath's Groove': 65 ft. HS (1946)
● **Froggatt-Curbar-Baslow Edges** (248 766 to 260 740): over 200 routes at 1000 ft altitude spread over 2 m. above Froggatt village. All standards, max. height 65 ft.
* 'Valkyrie': 65 ft. HVS (1948)
* 'Peapod': 65 ft. HVS (1951)
● **The Roaches** (002 630): two tiers of cliffs extending nearly ¾ m. at 1500 ft altitude some 4 m. N. of Leek. Over 70 climbs up to 100 ft, often of 2 or 3 pitches and working through many overhangs. Easy climbs tend to be short problems.
* 'The Sloth': 100 ft. HVS (1952)
* 'Black and Tans': 95 ft. S (1920)
● **Laddow Rocks** (056 012): some 300 yds of gaunt buttresses and steep chimneys at 1500 ft altitude on moors 3 m. E. of Tintwistle near Glossop. Max. height 100 ft, climbs often 2 or 3 pitches.
* 'Tower Face': 60 ft. VS (c. 1920)
* 'Long Climb': 105 ft. VD (c. 1920)
2 Limestone: steep cliffs of **carbon-iferous** (i.e. 'mountain') **limestone**

flank many of the river valleys in the White Peak; usually vertical or over-hanging and often quite extensive. Originally developed for aid-climbing but now high-standard free routes. Climbs typically bold, gymnastic, and very exposed, holds small and fragile, and rock often loose. Few climbs easy, most serious. Important crags include:
● **Matlock High Tor** (297 590): above wooded but semi-urban Derwent river valley ½ m. S. of Matlock. Many climbs of high standard on impressive 150-ft bastion; many others, often easier, on line of other cliffs close by in valley. Council property, so sometimes access problems.
* 'Debauchery': 220 ft. HVS (1965)
● **Stoney Middleton Dale** (224 757): series of great buttresses, parts of some once quarried, extend about ¾ m. along wooded valley shared with main road and some active quarries, immediately W. of Stoney Middleton village. About 70 climbs of between 100 and 250 ft include a few shorter easier ones.
* 'Windhover': 240 ft. HVS (1958)
● **Cheedale** (115 726 to 124 733): steep buttresses line southern side of attractive Wye gorge, sharing it with abandoned railway, some 3 m. E. of Buxton. Over 70 climbs include several shorter easier ones: heights 45–270 ft.
* 'Chee Tor Girdle': 650 ft. VS (1964)
● Spectacular climbs in **Dovedale** (e.g. pinnacles of Ilam Rock and Pickering Tor) and in **Manifold Valley** (e.g. Thor's Cave and Beeston Tor crags).

The Yorkshire Dales

Essential Information

Height: Average between 1500 and 1900 ft; max. Whernside (2416 ft)
Area: North–south 40 miles; east–west 35 miles
Distances from main towns: Leeds (centre) 15 miles; Harrogate 5 miles; York 25 miles
Suggested bases: Harrogate, Hawes, Ingleton
Access routes: A59 (south) between Harrogate and Skipton; B6160 (central) between Grassington and Aysgarth; B6270 (north) between Richmond and Kirkby Stephen
BR stations: Skipton, Settle, Ilkley
Youth hostels: Ingleton, Hawes, Aysgarth Falls, Keld, Malham, Ramsgill, Stainforth (total of 26 within Yorkshire region)
OS maps: 98, 99, 103, 104

The Yorkshire Dales cover some 680 square miles across the central Pennines, forming the third-largest National Park. It is a landscape of mountain and moorland, the gritstone fells covered with heather, rough grass, and sphagnum bogs. A massive geological upheaval, the Craven Fault, exposed the huge scars and limestone pavements which are one of the most remarkable features of the Dales. A vast network of caves and pot-holes has been eroded within the limestone over millions of years by the action of rainwater and rivers.

The heights are intersected by broad pastoral river valleys and fertile meadows. Innumerable streams and cascades rush down steep gills from the moorland watershed; in places, the streams broaden to waterfalls (or forces), of which Hardrow and Aysgarth are the most spectacular.

The Three Peaks

To many keen walkers, the Three Peaks – Pen-y-Ghent, Ingleborough, and Whernside – which dominate the landscape of the central Dales are

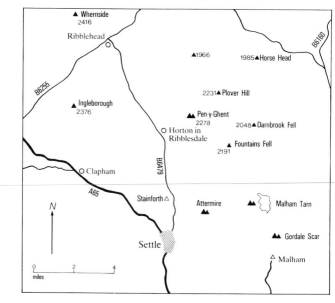

the epitome of walking in the Pennines. To traverse all three in one day represents the ultimate challenge, and in good weather they make a splendid expedition.

Horton in Ribblesdale is the most convenient base for access to Pen-y-Ghent (2278 feet), perhaps the most famous summit along the Pennine Way. The ascent up the smooth grassy slopes with their small limestone outcrops is not difficult; the walk along the ridge to the summit, rimmed with gritstone crags, gives splendid views in all directions.

To the west rises the square gritstone summit of Ingleborough (2376 feet) topped by four cairns. There are a number of recognized access routes, the best (of some 4 miles) starting from Clapham and following Clapham Beck to Ingleborough Cave, carved out of a massive limestone cliff. From here, the track continues via Gaping Gill, an immense 340-foot pothole, over boggy and sometimes steep terrain to the summit.

Whernside, the third of the Three Peaks and the highest point in the Yorkshire Dales (2416 feet), can be reached via a ridge path which starts from Ribblehead just north of Ingleborough. The 3-mile ascent is both easy and invigorating, and from the summit there are fine views of Pen-y-Ghent and Ingleborough rising to the east and south.

The whole of the Ribblesdale area offers much potential for hill-walking, climbing, and rock-scrambling. It is also a favourite centre for potholers who are keen to explore the famous Sell Gill Holes, Cross Pot, and Jackdaw Hole.

The steep, narrow defile of Swale Gorge below Kisdon Force.

Wensleydale

Wensleydale, which stretches almost due east–west for some 25 miles in the northern half of the area, is the broadest of the dales, and offers both beautiful scenery and good walking. Hawes is the recognized halfway point for walkers of the Pennine Way and several other tracks radiate from the village across the fells. Not far from Hawes is Hardrow Force, a spectacular waterfall with an uninterrupted drop of nearly 100 feet. In the eastern part of the dale, by the main A684 road, the River Ure forms the Aysgarth Forces, a succession of cascades which are particularly splendid when the river is in spate. Clearly defined paths lead to both of these waterfalls.

Swaledale

From Wensleydale, Buttertubs Pass leads into Swaledale to the north, arguably the most beautiful of the dales. The Pass crosses wild expanses of moorland between Great Shunner Fell (2349 feet) and Lovely Seat (2213 feet) before dropping into Swaledale which offers a variety of charming riverside walks through the hamlets of Muker, Thwaite, and Keld.

Malhamdale

Gargrave, where the Pennine Way enters the Dales National Park, is a good base from which to explore Malhamdale. Quite apart from the Way itself, which here includes pleasant riverside walking by the Aire, there is much to explore in the vicinity of Malham village. The 300-foot limestone cliffs of Malham Cove are a popular attraction, especially with rock-climbers; on the moors about 2 miles to the north lies the glacial Malham Tarn, reached by a footpath which crosses the remarkable limestone pavement above the Cove, the highest in the Pennines (1300 feet). Gordale

The precipitous walls of Gordale Scar.

Scar, about a mile north-east of Malham, a limestone ravine with towering 200-foot precipices, is considered by some even more spectacular than Malham Cove. Both Gordale and Malham are the strict preserve of experienced climbers.

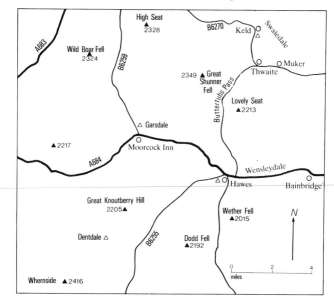

Climbing Information

Many cliffs, a few relatively large but many merely small 'scars' or outcrops. Two rock types:

1 Gritstone – good firm **millstone grit** – see under Peak District, p.29.

● **Almscliff** (268 490): a double-tiered tor ('High Man' and 'Low Man') on a hill-top overlooking Wharfedale, 5 m. SW. of Harrogate. 100-yd face of turreted walls, chimneys, and cracks some 50 ft. high provide over 60 climbs (all standards) and numerous problems on scattered boulders and pinnacles. Highly regarded. Open to the weather.

* 'Parsons' Chimney': 50 ft. HS (1900)

* 'Frankland's Green Crack': 45 ft. VS (c.1923)

● **Brimham Rocks** (209 650): towers and pinnacles, many of grotesque shape, in open, lightly wooded moorland. Climbs (all standards) up to about 60 ft, some to actual summits not entirely straightforward to descend. Also some 1000 yds of broken 'edge' close by gives more conventional gritstone climbs. Tourist venue but ideal for light-hearted climbing.

● **Pen-y-Ghent** (836 732): 2000 ft up close under summit of mountain in incredible situation 2 m. NE of Horton in Ribblesdale. 90-ft exposed buttress holds a dozen or so climbs from D to HVS. A crag unique outside major mountain areas.

* 'Red Pencil Direct': 90 ft. S (1956)

● **Ilkley Moor** (12 46): at 1200 ft altitude overlooking Lower Wharfedale ½ m. S. of Ilkley village. Celebrated Cow and Calf Rocks give short 'super-boulder' problems, fiercer climbs up to 50 ft in Quarry (**sandstone**) close by. Tourist venue.

● Among other gritstone cliffs, **Crookrise** (988 559), high on moor edge 2½ m. N. of Skipton, is one of the best. Many routes (all grades) up to 60 ft.

2 Carboniferous (i.e. 'mountain') **limestone** outcrops in many places. Much is loose and of interest only to local climbers but there are several larger cliffs of national interest.

Kilnsey Crag, Upper Wharfedale.

● **Malham Cove** (898 640): one of scenic wonders of Britain and thus popular tourist venue. Huge natural amphitheatre holds nearly 100 climbs, typically around 100 ft, and more exposed than length suggests. Rock said to be best limestone in Yorkshire. Few easy climbs tend to be short; most hard with several long aid lines (A3 – bolts).

* 'Carnage': 120 ft. HVS (1965)

● **Kilnsey Crag** (973 680): conspicuous crag of leaning buttresses and jutting overhangs close to valley floor in Upper Wharfedale 3 m. NW. of Grassington. Sheltered situation. Main feature is 30-ft horizontal roof above 70-ft bulging wall. No easy climbs, all are spectacular hard lines, many on aid. Rock typically compact. Involved in birth of British 'aid-climbing'.

* 'Main Overhang': 250 ft. A3 (1957)

● **Gordale Scar** (915 640): scenic wonder and tourist venue 1 m. NE. of Malham village. Spectacular narrow gorge with overhanging walls up to 220 ft high. Originally developed for aid-climbing, now several free routes ascend seemingly impregnable walls. Climbs only of top standards. Friable rock.

* 'Cave Route': 180 ft. A3 or XS (1956)

● Other worthwhile crags: **Bull Scar** (992 682): 3 m. S. of Kettlewell, with quantity of easier climbs up to 35 ft. **Attermire Scar** (841 644): 1½ m. NE. of Settle with some 30 climbs up to 50 ft (many easier grades). **Great Close Scar** (904 665): beside Malham Tarn, some 25 climbs up to 90 ft (many easier grades).

The North York Moors

Essential Information

Height: Average between 950 and 1300 ft; max. Urra Moor at Botton Head (1490 ft)

Area: North–south 17 miles; east–west 35 miles

Distances from main towns:
Scarborough 4 miles;
Middlesborough 7 miles;
York 20 miles; Harrogate 22 miles

Suggested bases: Helmsley, Pickering, Whitby

Access routes: A19(T) (west) between Thirsk and Osmotherley; A171 (west) between Scarborough and Whitby; A170 (south) between Pickering and Thirsk

BR stations: Northallerton, Thirsk, Scarborough, Whitby

Youth hostels: Helmsley, Wheeldale, Lockton, Osmotherley, Whitby, Westerdale (total of 26 within Yorkshire region)

OS maps: 93, 94, 99, 100, 101

Much of the North York Moors lies within the National Park which comprises some 550 square miles stretching from the Hambleton Hills in the west to the North Sea coast above Scarborough. The heartland of the area is dominated by wide, open, heather-covered moors, rising to 1490 feet in the Cleveland Hills, separated in the south by deeply incised dales. Within its compass there is a strongly contrasting variety of scenery: the bold, rugged coastline with the cliffs at Boulby the highest on the east coast, the lonely expanses of moorland, the lush green dales.

The moors are ideal walking terrain. A vast network of footpaths and bridleways provides over 1000 miles of public paths, and in addition a number of trails and way-marked walks have been established. The Cleveland Way runs for 93

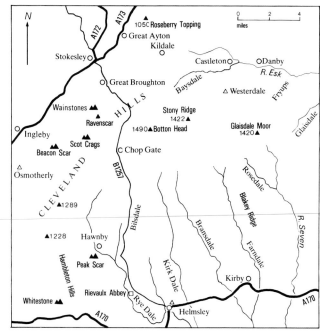

miles almost round the whole boundary of the Park, while the 40-mile Lyke Wake Walk crosses the central plateau from Osmotherley to Ravenscar. The walker in the North York Moors should be adequately prepared for sudden changes of temperature which are a common feature of the climate, which can be very severe. The coast is often cloaked in sea-mist, while thunder-storms are not infrequent over the moors.

The Hambleton Hills

The rich agricultural lands of the broad-topped Hambleton Hills form the western boundary of the area. Sutton Bank, an escarpment of the Hills some 5 miles east of Thirsk, rises to 960 feet above the surrounding plain and is a famous landmark for visitors entering the Park from the west. From the top of the steep cliff there are fine views over Gormire Lake and Hood Hill and back across the Vale of York. Near by to the south is the creamy limestone crag of Roulston Scar with the 315-foot-long Kilburn White Horse. A section of the Cleveland Way runs over the top of Sutton Bank.

The Cleveland Hills and northern moors

The Cleveland Hills, which lie in a wide curve to the north of the Hambleton Hills, include the highest ground in the region on Urra Moor (1490 feet). Glaisdale Moor is one of several moorland tracts that radiate to the east of the Cleveland Hills,

View south from the summit of Whitestone cliff over Gormire Lake.

including Bransdale, Farndale, Westerdale, Baysdale, and Rosedale.

The terrain around Glaisdale, just to the north of Rosedale, offers invigorating walking: south along the River Seven, or north over an old railway route across Blakey Ridge above the River Dove, with 1000 feet of elevation in each direction. Five miles south of Egton Bridge at Goathland village there is also an extremely well-preserved stretch of the Roman military road known as Wade's Causeway which once extended for 25 miles over Wheeldale Moor.

The northern moors above the Esk Valley are equally inviting. A strategic starting-point is Danby Lodge, one of the Park's Information Centres. From here there is good access to the austere heights of Danby Dale, Great and Little Fryup Dale, and Westerdale. There is much evidence of prehistoric settlement on the high ground, in the many burial mounds and stone cairns scattered along the long, narrow ridges (or riggs) between the dales.

A few miles north of the

Ralph Cross on Danby High Moor.

Cleveland Hills stands Roseberry Topping, its 1050-foot summit a landmark on the northern edge of the Park. Although scarred by inten-

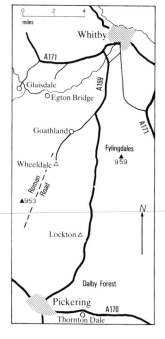

36

Rosedale, from Rosedale Head (1350 feet).

sive mining and quarrying over the centuries, the hill is a worthwhile objective as a fine viewpoint.

The southern valleys

The dales in the southern part of the National Park present softer, pastoral scenery of farmland and woodland. The secluded river valleys of Rye Dale, Kirk Dale, and Farndale are all richly fertile; Farndale in particular is famous for its display of wild daffodils in the spring. Extensive forests have been planted between Pickering and Scarborough, restoring some of the plantations that were once an important part of the north Yorkshire landscape. Dalby Forest, 4 miles northeast of Pickering near Thornton Dale, contains a number of way-marked trails and is rich in interesting flora and fauna.

Rye Dale is dominated by the imposing ruins of the thirteenth-century Rievaulx Abbey. The Cleveland Way crosses the Dale to the south of Rievaulx from its starting-point at Helmsley.

Climbing Information

1 Jurassic **sandstone**/ironstone: more than 20 scattered crags, usually edges on lip of moor at around 900-ft contour. Typically climbs are of all grades, 40–50 ft in length. Many shorter boulder problems. Best known are twin crags at Hasty Bank, 4 m. SE. of Stokesley.

● **Wainstones** (559 036): some 60 climbs up to 45 ft, many at VD and S on shattered boulders and grotesque towers.

● **Ravenscar** (566 037): more awesome with some 50 fiercer climbs up to 85 ft.

Other crags include **Highcliff Nab** (610 138), **Scot Crags** (520 004), **Beacon Scar** (460 998), and concentration of smaller crags on moor edges to E. and SE. of Great Ayton (560 109) including one high on **Roseberry Topping** – the 'Matterhorn of Cleveland'.

2 Jurassic **limestone**: two excellent vertical crags of typically clean but rather friable rock.

● **Whitestone Cliff** (507 836): finely situated on Cleveland Way 5 m. E. of Thirsk on 1000-ft contour overlooking Vale of York. Some 40 climbs up to 120 ft, mostly VS or harder.

**'Nightwatch': 110 ft. HS (1962)

● **Peak Scar** (527 884): in sheltered wooded valley above Upper Ryedale. Some 50 climbs up to 100 ft, mostly VS or harder.

Forest of Bowland

Essential Information

Height: Average between 1300 and 1700 ft; max. Mallowdale Fell (1840 ft)
Area: North–south 14 miles; east–west 18 miles
Distances from main towns: Lancaster 4 miles; Preston 10 miles; Blackpool 15 miles
Suggested base: Clitheroe
Access routes: M6 (west), exit 33; B6478 (east) between Clitheroe and Long Preston; A683 (north) east of Lancaster, then B6480
BR stations: Lancaster, High Bentham, Clitheroe
Youth hostel: Slaidburn
OS maps: 102, 103

The Forest of Bowland, which covers 300 square miles to the north of industrial Lancashire, is a forest in name only, and actually encompasses some of the most spectacular moorland in Britain. A great part of its appeal lies in its solitude and privacy, all the more precious given its geographical proximity to the busy Fylde coast.

The northern part of the area consists of stern gritstone fells; the high ridge of Bowland Knotts marks the northern boundary on the border between Lancashire and North Yorkshire. In the south the landscape is broken by secluded dales and rushing streams, by isolated villages and farmsteads in fertile meadows.

Trough of Bowland

The wild pass of the Trough of Bowland, which stretches for some 12 miles from Quernmore, near Lancaster, southeast to Dunsop Bridge, epitomizes all that is best in the area. The road through the pass crosses lonely moorland and fells, relieved by wooded glades and water-courses.

In the far north-western corner rises Clougha Pike, its summit offering wide views as far as the Lakeland hills. There

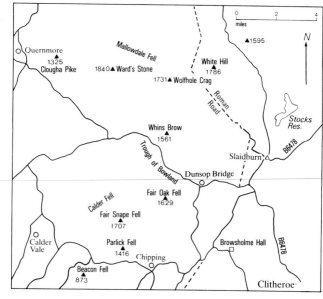

Trough of Bowland: from the crest of the pass towards Dunsop Bridge.

are many opportunities for exhilarating walking expeditions along the whole length of the Trough: Ward's Stone on Mallowdale Fell, the highest point in Bowland (1840 feet); the valley of Rams Clough leading to the 1400-foot summit of Whin Fell.

The southern fells

Chipping is a convenient centre from which to explore the southern fells, including Fairoak Fell, Wolf Fell, and Fair Snape Fell. One splendid local excursion is the ascent of Parlick Fell which looms to the northwest of the village. Although the climb is steep, it is infinitely rewarding, as the views from the summit (1416 feet) extend for miles around, northwards to the Lake District, southwards to Snowdonia, and in good weather conditions even as far as the Isle of Man in the west.

There are more wide views from the top of Beacon Fell (873 feet), on the southern edge of Bowland. It is an easy climb through thick woods to the wide summit covered with moor-grass, heather, and wild berries.

More demanding, and higher, ground lies to the north of Chipping. Fair Snape Fell rises to 1707 feet, and beyond is the great flank of Calder Fell. From Calder a footpath leads through lush woodland to Nicky Nook, a famous beauty spot.

Pendle Hill

The bare hill of Pendle, covering 25 square miles due east of Clitheroe, an ancient and charming market town, dominates the far south-eastern corner of the area. Numerous paths lead up the steep flanks of the hill, but the effort of the ascent to the 1827-foot summit is rewarded by the panoramic views from the vast gritstone plateau.

Hill Ranges

Britain has such a vast variety of hill ranges that it would take the walker several lifetimes to cover them all. Suffice it to say that wherever one lives in these islands, hill-walking of the most pleasing and rejuvenating kind is never far away. First-time walkers to Norfolk, for instance, are frequently surprised at the coastal heights around Sheringham and Kelling Heath. Those venturing among the Yorkshire Wolds above Lincolnshire will find hills of gentle aspect which nevertheless offer rewarding walks. These are the quiet hills, ideal for novices intent on trying more demanding heights at some future date.

This section includes a wide geographical selection ranging from the gentlest, where both access and the going are easy, to those that only fall short of mountains by the smallest of margins, if at all. The latter are challenging enough to tempt the fittest and most eager of walkers.

The problem of differentiating between a hill and a

1 The Mendips
2 The Cotswold Hills
3 The Malvern Hills
4 The Shropshire Hills
5 The Chilterns
6 The Clwydians
7 Eastern Cumbria and Durham
8 Northumberland
9 The Lammermuir and Moorfoot Hills
10 The Ochil Hills
11 The Lowther Hills to Glen Trool

mountain is difficult in the context of Britain. In England and Wales – the Lake District and Snowdonia apart – the hill and mountain ranges are not clearly divided. Just to confuse things further, the Scots call all their peaks 'hills', even mighty Ben Nevis and the giant Cairngorms. There is an arbitrary yardstick which declares that any British hill exceeding 2000 feet qualifies as a mountain. Yet many would question the name 'hills' used to describe the Clwydian range in Wales (especially those who have tramped these wild heights), which in fact nowhere exceed 1900 feet.

It is precisely this complexity of landscape which makes Britain so appealing to the walker. There is hill scenery to suit every taste and every level of expertise. The novice negotiating a ridge of the Chilterns will be as richly rewarded as the veteran traversing the wild Lammermuirs or Cheviots of the Scottish Borders.

Practical Points

● Never underestimate hill contours which are often deceptively gentle from a distance. Even the most compact group of hills (like the Malverns) will take a toll from under-used leg-muscles.

● To conserve energy keep to the same contour line where possible, rather than zigzagging up and down. This applies particularly when distance-walking in wilder hills (as in Northumberland), where footpaths are seldom well marked or prolific.

● Paradoxically, it is often almost as tiring on the muscles to descend as to ascend, especially towards the end of an energetic day with long descents to be tackled. Do not hurry the descent or front thigh muscles may tighten, which will incapacitate you for the next day.

● Navigation is not quite so vital on southern hills since elevation provides commanding views of a landscape usually well endowed with pockets of civilization. In the north, Wales, and Scotland, however, constant reference to map and compass may be needed. Keep in practice anyway, even when direction is obvious, just in case visibility closes down quickly.

● Many, if not most, hill ranges of Britain are open-air classrooms for students of geology, natural history, or prehistory. Wider interest is awakened through further field-study of one or preferably all of these subjects, which do become more absorbing the more one delves.

● On any two-day hill walk, or longer, try to select an overnight location on high ground if possible (inn, camp ground, youth hostel, etc.). Valley accommodation may be cosy and beckoning but in the early morning metabolism is usually low – no time to make a stiff, prolonged climb back to the tops, especially with a well-loaded rucksack.

The Mendips

Essential Information

Height: Average between 900 and 1000 ft; max. Black Down (1067 ft)
Area: North-west to south-east 19 miles; north-east to south-west 5 miles
Distances from main towns: Weston-super-Mare 7 miles; Bristol (central) 12 miles
Suggested bases: Cheddar, Wells
Access routes: M5 (west), exit 21; A37 (east) north of Shepton Mallet; A371 (south) between Wells and Cheddar; B3135 (central) for Cheddar Gorge
BR stations: Weston-super-Mare, Frome
Youth hostels: Cheddar, Street
OS maps: 172, 182, 183

The limestone mass of the Mendip Hills stretches for some 30 miles across the northern boundary of Somerset, dropping away to Salisbury Plain in the east. The most outstanding, and most well-known, feature of the area is the extensive network of cliffs and underground caverns that have been carved out of the limestone by the action of water over thousands of years. It is a bleak and lonely land-scape, criss-crossed by ancient tracks and roads, with numerous settlements and burial mounds which testify to the historical importance of the region.

Cheddar Gorge

The most famous areas in the Mendips are without doubt Cheddar Gorge and Wookey Hole Caves. One way to see Cheddar Gorge while avoiding the tourist crowds in the summer is to park at Black Rock Gate just to the north-east and take the 450-foot-high cliff-top path to the village, descending via Jacob's Ladder. The views from the top of the cliffs are exhilarating, over such high spots as Horseshoe Bend, the Pinnacles, and Lion Rock.

Quiet and secluded contrast to Cheddar Gorge can be found near by, at Black Rock and Ebbor Gorge. The sheltered valley of Black Rock, less than 2 miles to the north-east, offers walking in a setting of great natural beauty, tracing an ancient Roman trail. Ebbor

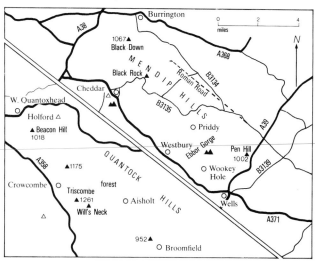

Gorge, between Wells and Cheddar, is widely considered to be the most unspoiled part of the area. It is especially important for its wealth of Stone Age relics.

Black Down

The highest point in the Mendips, Black Down (1067 feet), rises above the limestone plateau north-east of Cheddar. The sandstone summit – distinguished from the main mass of the range by the different vegetation which covers it – can be reached by a variety of paths starting from Ellick House near Burrington. There are fine panoramic views from the top.

The Quantocks

The Quantocks, the second of Somerset's hill ranges, lie some 20 miles south-west of the Mendip Hills. Although only small in area – extending for 12 miles south-east from the Bristol Channel and at no point wider than 4 miles – they comprise a beautiful landscape of gently rolling hills covered in woodland or heather, cut by deep combes. An ancient ridgeway route runs the whole length of the hills, giving pleasant and easy walking.

Will's Neck

At the heart of the region lies Aisholt Common, a moorland plateau to the south of Quantock Forest. A nature trail has been laid out over the Common, giving fine and varying views. The trail ends with the ascent to the 1260-foot ridge of Will's Neck, the highest point in the Quantocks. There is an alternative route to the summit by a footpath from Triscombe Stone, south-east of Crowcombe.

Climbing Information

All climbing is on **carboniferous** (i.e. 'mountain') **limestone** and is typical of that rock, usually vertical with small fragile holds and abundant loose material. Harder routes are serious and require experience to be climbed safely.

● **Cheddar Gorge** (470 542): over ½ m. extremely spectacular cliffs up to 430 ft, tallest limestone cliffs in UK and very important climbing area. Popular tourist venue, thus climbing forbidden Easter–September. Over 100 climbs, all serious, from easier shorter ones to long top-grade modern routes; all very steep and exposed, many problems with loose rock and ivy.
* 'Coronation Street': 400 ft. HVS (1965)
* 'Knights Climb': 210 ft. D (1931)

● **Brean Down**: immediately south of Weston-super-Mare. Some 50 climbs, traverses and problems of all standards accessible except at high tide on several crags along a mile of south-facing coast. Max. height 100 ft.
* 'Great Corner': 100 ft. HVS (1975)

● Short climbs at several outcroppings and quarries in the region, notably **Churchill Rocks** (446 592) and **Ebbor Gorge** (529 489).

● **Avon Gorge** (56 73 and 56 74): although 12 m. north of Mendip, included because same rock and most popular climbing area in South. Three main areas of cliff, two long-abandoned quarries and one natural, along west-facing flank of narrow valley of R. Avon below Clifton Downs and within 1½ m. Bristol City Centre. Semi-urban environment above busy main road but nevertheless excellent and enjoyable climbing. Some 150 routes, up to 280 vertical ft (all grades), typically on open faces and walls: many modern vertical top-grade climbs but some easier on slabs. Peg belays usual, protection often poor. Rock mostly good.
* 'The Arete' + 'Direct Route': 230 ft. VD (1930s)
* 'Giant's Cave Buttress': 280 ft. VS (1950s)
* 'Malbogies': 200 ft. HVS (1959)

The Cotswold Hills

Essential Information

Height: Average between 800 and 950 ft; max. Cleeve Hill (1083 ft)
Area: North-east to south-west 39 miles; north-west to south-east 10 miles
Distances from main towns: Cheltenham 4 miles; Gloucester 5 miles; Bristol 16 miles
Suggested bases: Cheltenham, Evesham, Stow-on-the-Wold
Access routes: M5 (west), exit 11; A429 (east) between Cirencester and Stow-on-the-Wold; B4070 (south central) between Stroud and Birdlip; B4077 (north central) between Stow and Stanway
BR stations: Stroud, Gloucester, Cheltenham
Youth hostels: Duntisbourne Abbots, Cleeve Hill (Cheltenham), Stow-on-the-Wold
OS maps: 150, 162, 163, 172, 173

The Cotswold Hills stretch for some 60 miles from Bath northeast to Broadway, part of the vast belt of limestone thrown up as a result of geological activity over 10 million years ago. The main part of the area lies in Gloucestershire, but the Cotswolds also include corners of Avon, Oxfordshire, and Hereford & Worcester.

The limestone has characterized the whole aspect of the area. It is a fertile landscape of undulating hills crossed by drystone walls, of deep woodland, of villages and townships of honey-coloured stone. In the west, the exposed outcrops of the escarpment drop into the wooded vales of Evesham, Gloucester, and Berkeley; in the east, the hills roll down to the Oxfordshire plain.

A variety of trails wander through the hills, all of them scenic and some following historic routes. The Cotswold Way runs for 100 miles from Bath to Chipping Camden. Other routes overlie old drove roads and salt roads.

The northern Cotswolds

The main heights lie in the north, affording wide views

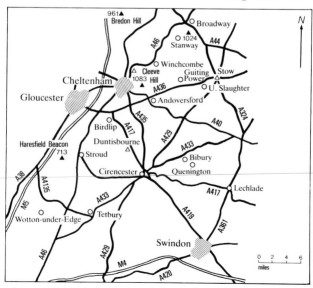

over the escarpment into the surrounding valleys. Broadway Hill (1024 feet), to the south-east of Broadway, looks out over the Vale of Evesham and beyond to the Black Mountains; there is easy access to the summit by a variety of footpaths from the village. The limestone outcrop of Bredon Hill (961 feet) rises 6 miles south-west of Evesham; a massive Iron Age hill-fort, Kemerton Camp, crowns the summit.

Cleeve Hill

The Cotswolds rise to their highest point 3 miles north-east of Cheltenham, on the 1083-foot ridge of Cleeve Cloud, just to the south-east of Cleeve Hill. From this view-point wide panoramas extend in all directions, as far as the Brecon Beacons over 40 miles away in the west. From Cleeve Hill a path runs over Cleeve Common to Belas Knap, a massive Stone Age long barrow. Cleeve Common, and Cleeve Cloud, can be reached via the A46 from Winchcombe.

The central and southern Cotswolds

The central and southern Cotswolds offer walking of a different kind. Around Wotton-under-Edge, along the Westridge spur of the escarpment, there is fine walking through 2000 acres of woodland, and near by are many lovely combes and valleys (The Bottoms). Rodborough Common above Stroud offers 800 acres of high open ground with views over the Stroud Valley. The 700-foot-high Haresfield Beacon, within the beautiful upland area of Standish Wood to the south of Gloucester, is one of the finest, and most popular,

Haresfield Beacon, viewed from Standish Hill.

viewpoints on the southern edge of the Cotswolds.

The lush valleys of the central Cotswold plateau contain many beautiful and often secluded corners, all worthy of exploration. From Bibury, in the Coln Valley, a pleasant river-side path runs through water-meadows to the village of Quenington, some 6 miles away. The Windrush Valley offers charming river-side walks near Upper and Lower Slaughter; in its upper reaches, just south of Kineton, is Guiting Power, a typical, and unspoiled, Cotswold village.

Climbing Information

The outcrops, usually once quarried, of **oolitic limestone** that occur here and there along the scarp edges are generally too rotten to provide serious climbing: nevertheless, there is some, typically vertical with very loose finishes. All three crags mentioned are in superb situations.

● **Cleeve Cloud** (984 262) at 1000 ft altitude overlooking Cheltenham. Several areas, best is Castle Rock, several climbs up to 35 ft and a couple of good traverses. Some belay stakes in position at top.

● **Leckhampton Hill** (946 183): notable for 'Devil's Chimney' rock tower with several lines, 20 ft, D to VD but serious in descent.

● **Haresfield Beacon** (828 083): a small crag of above average rock some 20 ft high and 40 yds long holds several 'fun' lines.

The Malvern Hills

Essential Information

Height: Average between 950 and 1200 ft; max. Worcestershire Beacon (1394 ft)
Area: North–south 10 miles; east–west ¾ mile
Distances from main towns: Worcester 8 miles; Hereford 15 miles; Birmingham (centre) 29 miles
Suggested base: Great Malvern
Access routes: A449 from Worcester (north), or Ledbury and Malvern Wells (south); M5 (east), exit 7 or 8
BR station: Great Malvern
Youth hostel: Malvern Hills
OS map: 150

The narrow 9-mile-long ridge of the Malvern Hills, formed of ancient volcanic rock some 600 million years old, rises steeply from the eastern Severn Valley along the former Hereford & Worcester border. The rugged northern end of the ridge gives way to lower, wooded summits of gentler, less stern aspect in the south below Herefordshire Beacon.

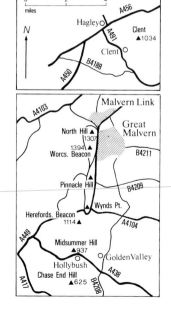

The hills have had a long and important history from pre-historic times when their lofty summits provided strategic defensive vantage points. Artists have found inspiration on the wooded slopes, and the wells of spring water made the area popular as a spa. The Malvern Hills offer splendid walking terrain throughout the year, their beauty varying only with the season; they are at their most colourful in autumn when the bracken is a blazing russet. A variety of paths cross the hills, some presenting ascents more taxing than the inexperienced walker might expect.

Worcestershire Beacon

This highest of the six main summits in the Malvern range rises to 1394 feet just west of Great Malvern. Great Malvern is a strategic starting-point for any ascent to the broad, well-marked path that runs along the full length of the summit ridge. From the town the path climbs to North Hill (1307 feet), the northernmost summit, and continues to the Worcestershire Beacon. On a clear day the views are truly panoramic, extending over 15 counties.

The path follows the undulating ridge, swooping down through Wyche Cutting, ascending Pinnacle Hill with its three summits, dropping into Wynds Point gap, and then climbing up to Herefordshire Beacon at 1114 feet. The massive prehistoric earthworks of British Camp cover 32 acres on the broad summit of the hill.

The southern summits

The round wooded flank of Broad Down to the immediate south of Herefordshire Beacon

*Midsummer Hill with
Chase End Hill beyond.*

is the first of the gentler southern summits. An Iron Age hill-fort crowns the two peaks of Midsummer and Hollybush Hills above the hamlet of Hollybush further south, and there is yet more pleasant walking across Raggedstone Hill above Golden Valley and Chase End Hill at the end of the range.

The Clent Hills

In addition to the Malverns, in the heart of England, understandably popular with walkers in the Midlands conurbations, there are the Worcestershire Clent Hills. Scarcely 12 miles from Birmingham city centre,

they offer a wide choice of footpaths through truly lovely scenery. This compact range covers the two main heights of the Clent and Walton Hills, rising to above 1000 feet; from the summit of Walton Hill it is possible to see the Welsh peaks on a clear day. Access to these beautiful, and ancient, uplands is from Clent village off the main A491, 6 miles from Bromsgrove.

Climbing Information

Climbs have been made on the compact **igneous** rock of several small outcrops and old quarries along the chain of hills. Notably at **The Gullet** (762 382), **Pinnacle Hill** (769 413), and **North Hill** (770 469).

The Shropshire Hills

Essential Information

Height: Average between 1100 and 1500 ft; max. Brown Clee Hill (1790 ft)
Area: North-west to south-east 22 miles; north-east to south-west 16 miles
Distances from main towns: Shrewsbury 8 miles; Wolverhampton 22 miles; Birmingham 35 miles
Suggested bases: Ludlow, Church Stretton, Much Wenlock
Access routes: A49 (south and central) via Ludlow; A488 (north and west) via Shrewsbury; A458 and A4371 (east) via Much Wenlock
BR stations: Church Stretton, Craven Arms, Ludlow
Youth hostels: Ludlow, Bridges, Wheathill, Wilderhope, Clun Mill
OS maps: 126, 127, 137, 138

Veteran hill-walkers are well aware of what Shropshire has to offer. The 300 square miles of this area of outstanding natural beauty are a worthy alternative to other, more popular hill ranges in high summer, if invigorating walking amid tranquillity is sought after.

It is an ancient landscape already settled by Stone Age tribes. The geological substance of the hills is more ancient still: the volcanic bed-rock of The Wrekin is estimated to be some 900 million years old.

Brown Clee Hill

The Clee Hills in the eastern part of the region contain the highest of the Shropshire summits: Brown Clee Hill (1790 feet). The hill can be reached via the established forest trail which begins just outside the village of Cleobury North; or from the parking places beyond Abdon on the minor road off the B4364. There are three hillforts on the slopes of Brown Clee, the most impressive being Nordybank.

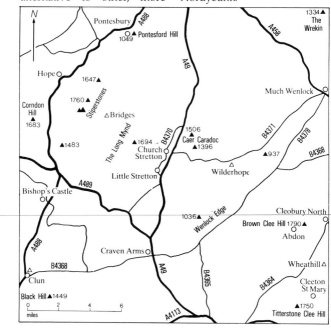

Wenlock Edge

The steep limestone escarpment of Wenlock Edge stretches in an unbroken diagonal line for some 16 miles across the centre of the county from Much Wenlock to Craven Arms. The quarries in the northern part give way to deep woodland, part of it a nature reserve. Access to the Edge is along the B4371 from Much Wenlock or the B4368 and B4378 from Craven Arms. Numerous paths and trails run up the slopes to the summit plateau (950 feet) which is dotted with ancient remains. Although it is not very high, the Edge affords splendid views.

To the north of Wenlock Edge and divided from the main hill ranges stands The Wrekin (1334 feet). Its isolated position makes it a prominent, and famous, landmark for miles around, and at the same time ensures a panoramic view from the summit. The path to the summit and the Iron Age fort (c. 200 BC) starts from the minor road on the eastern side of the hill.

The Long Mynd

The rounded ridge of The Long Mynd which extends for 6 miles to the west of Church Stretton is probably the prime attraction for hill-walkers in Shropshire. It is one of the most individual upland ranges in Britain, an area of wild moorland cut by deep, narrow valleys, which appears higher than its maximum of 1700 feet. The Long Mynd offers excellent walking on a wide choice of footpaths. It can be reached via minor roads adjoining the B4370 from the town of Church Stretton.

To the east of The Long Mynd rise the seven Stretton Hills (or Caradoc range); like The Wrekin their rocks are of volcanic origin. Caer Caradoc is the highest summit in the range (1506 feet). A variety of easy paths climb to the tops which give wide views.

Shropshire's hills offer markedly contrasting scenery. The Stiperstones, 5 miles north-west of The Long Mynd, are an austere ridge of jagged crags and strangely shaped rock formations. There are several access routes, the easiest by a path which starts beyond the village of Bridges. A 3-mile-long path traverses the summit ridge (1762 feet); in clear conditions the Welsh mountains can be seen rising to the west.

Climbing Information

Outcrops of compact **igneous** rock occur at places in the hills. Notable:

● **Pontesford Rocks** (409 049) on slopes of Earls Hill (990 ft) above Pontesbury village some 7 m. SW. of Shrewsbury. East Buttress, West Buttress, and Pontesbury Needle, separated by grassy gullies, rise steeply some 200 ft high from wooded slopes. More than 20 climbs (mostly easier grades).
* 'Varsity Buttress': 210 ft. S.
* 'Finale Groove': 200 ft. S. (c. 1958)

● **Stiperstones**: a line of **quartzite** pinnacles along the hill crest some 1700 ft up and open to the wind and weather. Highest, 'Devil's Chair' (369 992), some 50 ft high provides some scrambling.

● Various quarries e.g. Lawrence Hill Quarry on the **Wrekin** (62 08), loose climbs up to 200 ft.

● Climbs have also been made at various outcrops of soft **sandstone** e.g. **Nesscliff Hill** (384 195) where vertical 80-ft cliffs have provided some intimidating climbs. Another is **High Rock** in the Severn gorge at Bridgenorth.

The Chilterns

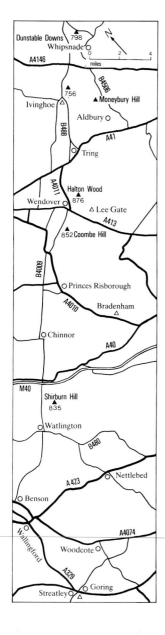

Essential Information

Height: Average between 600 and 750 ft; max. Wendover Woods (876 ft)
Area: North-east to south-west 25 miles; north-west to south-east 4 miles
Distances from main towns: Reading 7 miles; Luton 9 miles; London (central) 33 miles
Suggested bases: Watlington, Streatley-on-Thames, Henley-on-Thames
Access routes: A423 or M40 (south), exit 5; A4010 (central); A413 (north)
BR stations: Goring-on-Thames, Princes Risborough, Tring
Youth hostels: Streatley-on-Thames, Henley-on-Thames, Bradenham, Lee Gate, Ivinghoe
OS maps: 165, 166, 175

The chalky slopes of the Chiltern Hills are the most gentle of England's hill ranges: neat, smooth, and covered with deep beechwoods and lush pastures. They are easily accessible from London and provide a good training-ground for walkers as the entire length of the Chiltern ridge is traced by the Ridgeway long-distance path. Extending for 50 miles from Goring in the south-west to Sharpenhoe beyond Luton, over parts of Oxfordshire, Buckinghamshire, Hertfordshire, and Bedfordshire, these historic hills contain more than 100 recorded prehistoric sites.

Since the mid-sixties some 300 square miles of the Chilterns have been designated an area of outstanding natural beauty. The great natural splendour of the hills is to be found in the deep combes which break up the line of the scarp, usually clad in the most majestic beech trees. In the nineteenth century the Chilterns were a great centre of English furniture-making, and this resulted in continual tree-planting. Today some 30 000 acres of these beech-clad hills still remain, despite the spread of urban development and new roads.

Woodland summits

There is endless fine walking in the whole of the Chilterns area, for both the experienced walker and the novice, and some of the best is through the beech-woods. Burnham Beeches, some 500 acres to the south of Beaconsfield, are possibly the most famous, but there is further beautiful woodland around Shirburn Hill, north-east of Watlington, which is crossed by the ancient Icknield Way. A network of paths radiate over Christmas Common, about a mile from Shirburn Hill, leading to high view-points.

The Chilterns rise to their highest point in Wendover Woods, to the north-east of Wendover which lies in one of the five valleys ('gaps') which cut the Chiltern ridge. The summit cairn at 876 feet stands on the edge of Halton Wood. Many way-marked trails and walks run through the woods,

emerging at high vantage points which give uninterrupted views across the surrounding countryside. A splendid view over the Vale of Aylesbury is obtained from the summit of Coombe Hill (852 feet), south-west of Wendover.

The northern part of the Chilterns is every bit as beautiful as the central and southern areas. From the lovely village of Aldbury, 3 miles east of Tring, a path leads up on to the beech-clad ridge of Moneybury Hill and across Aldbury Common. Ashridge Woods extend to the north, the outer bank of the Chiltern forest. Nature trails and footpaths run through the woods, giving outstanding views. To the north again rises the bare summit of Ivinghoe Beacon, or Beacon Hill (756 feet), which looks out over the Aylesbury plain and to Dunstable Downs in the east; Ivinghoe Beacon marks the northern end of the Ridgeway path.

Coombe Hill, south-west of Wendover, overlooking the Vale of Aylesbury.

The Clwydians

Essential Information

Height: Average between 1300 and 1500 ft; max. Moel Fammau (1820 ft)
Area: North–south 20 miles; east–west 10 miles
Distances from main towns: Chester 12 miles; Liverpool 35 miles
Suggested base: Denbigh
Access routes: A541 (east and north) between Wrexham and Bodfari; A525 (south) between Wrexham and Ruthin
BR stations: Wrexham, Prestatyn
Youth hostels: Maeshafn, Llangollen
OS maps: 116, 117

The Clwydians are the first hill range of any significance encountered by the visitor entering north-east Wales from Cheshire. Though comparatively little known, these fine hills comprise a continuous – and often very impressive – upland scarp, especially along the western flank between Llangollen and the coastal

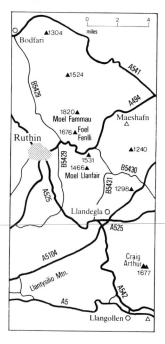

resort of Prestatyn. These once completely open heights are now being increasingly covered with conifer plantations by the Forestry Commission, but their essentially wild and wide character is none the less retained, despite the proximity of industrial Deeside.

Offa's Dyke Path

The main route across the Clwydian range is provided by a stretch of Offa's Dyke Path, the long-distance footpath that traces the frontier between Wales and England. The path climbs up to the Clwydian heights and runs over the main summits, providing fine panoramic views. Those walking the southern stretch in particular, between Llandegla and Bodfari, will find themselves in a very different, almost timeless, world as they traverse Moel-y-Plas, Moel Llanfair, and Moel Eithinen. Moel Fammau, 'Mother Hill', is aptly named as it is the highest point of the Clwydian range (1820 feet), and the most impressive. It is distinguished by the ruins of the tower erected to celebrate the Jubilee of George III.

From the wind-swept heather-clad height of Moel Fammau the distant mountains of Snowdonia stand out sharply on a clear day. However, such views are hard earned by the walker as the going involved in the 17 miles of successive hills is certainly strenuous. In between the summits are great swathes of open moorland, forestry plantations, and a number of Iron Age hill-forts. The massive remaining banks and ditches of Foel Fenlli (1676 feet), north-west of Moel Eithinen, is one of the best preserved relics. The

Clwydians beyond Denbighshire moors.

path drops eventually to the valley of the River Wheeler and Bodfari village, where most walkers arriving from Llandegla are glad to seek overnight accommodation.

North of Bodfari the long-distance path is easier, if more intricate, and involves a fair amount of lane-walking. There are nevertheless a number of high spots, limestone outcrops and caves, hill-forts like Moel-y-Gaer, together with a succession of woods, hill farms, and hamlets. The final scarp, high above Prestatyn, is dramatic, and memorable for those who have completed the full length of Offa's Dyke.

Near Denbigh, an ideal walking base.

Climbing Information

Two good cliffs of **carboniferous limestone** occur in the region among several small scrappy outcrops.

● **Craig y Forwen** (907 767): east-facing escarpment over 300 yds long above pretty valley of R. Dulas, 1 m. S. of Llandulas near Abergele. Over 50 climbs (all grades between VD and XS) up to 160 ft long, although mostly around 100 ft. Very steep but typically sound rock in a pleasant situation at only 200 ft above sea-level. Much recent development and a popular modern crag.
* 'Scalar': 120 ft. VS (1962)

● **Craig Arthur** (223 472): prominent west-facing buttress at 1200 ft above beautiful Eglwyseg Valley some 3 m. N. of Llangollen. Some 400 yds of cliff up to 120 ft high give very steep, indeed often overhanging, routes of great exposure, mostly in the higher grades.
*'Girdle Traverse': 900 ft. VS. (1969)

This limestone escarpment actually extends over 4 m. around the W. and SW. lips of Eglwyseg and Ruabon Mountains and offers many other climbing areas, some of which (as at Trevor) are long-abandoned quarries.

Eastern Cumbria and Durham

Essential Information

Height: Average between 1600 and 1850 ft; max. Cross Fell (2930 ft)
Area: North-west to south-east 35 miles; east–west 25 miles
Distances from main towns: Penrith 9 miles; Carlisle 17 miles; Middlesbrough 26 miles
Suggested bases: Penrith, Appleby, Barnard Castle

Access routes: A66 (south and west) between Bowes and Penrith; A689 (north and east) between Bishop Aukland and Alston; B6277 (centre) between Barnard Castle and Alston
BR stations: Appleby, Penrith, Bishop Aukland
Youth hostels: Dufton, Alston, Kirkby Stephen, Langdon Beck, Clove Lodge, Barnard Castle
OS maps: 87, 88, 90, 91, 92, 93

Eastern Cumbria

The northern section of the Pennines in eastern Cumbria to the east of the Eden Valley is a remote, unspoiled region where the walker can still find solitude in high places. To the north of the limestone belt which crosses the central Pen-

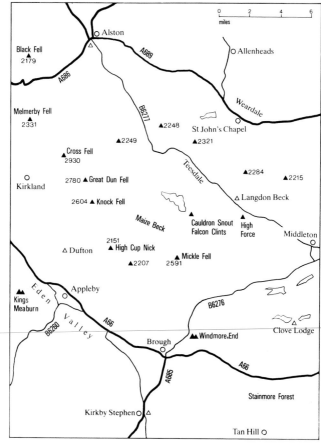

nines there extend vast expanses of high peat moorland which rise to culminate in the highest point in the Pennines on Cross Fell.

This desolate moorland scene immediately strikes the visitor, even from a road, but it is only the walker who will discover its real beauty. It is difficult and stern terrain rightly the preserve of the experienced. Without doubt, the best way to explore this area is to follow a section of the Pennine Way which here turns west from Teesdale in Durham across a corner of eastern Cumbria.

The scene is dramatic enough to the west of Cauldron Snout over high moorland along Maize Beck, then becomes quite spectacular at High Cup Nick some 4 miles east of Dufton. A clear track at an easy gradient leads from Dufton to the gigantic chasm of High Cup Nick (2151 feet). The precipitous dolerite cliffs with their peculiar, jagged formation drop sheer to the floor of the chasm. From the rim of the precipices there is a good view over the Vale of Eden to the Lakeland hills.

Cross Fell

North of Dufton looms Cross Fell (2930 feet), half hidden by the neighbouring Knock Fell, Great Dun Fell, and Skirwith Fell. It is bounded on the southwest by Kirkland Fell, which is distinguished by the crags of Wildboar Scar, but on its other sides stretches boggy moorland. The summit affords commanding views northwards to the Cheviots and southwards to the Yorkshire peaks.

Durham

The county of Durham is also rich in natural grandeur. Much of the terrain west of the Consett–Darlington industrial belt is of outstanding beauty; the rugged moorland in the west and the wooded banks of Teesdale both hold a strong appeal for walkers.

Barnard Castle is a strategic base from which to explore Teesdale and Weardale. The finest scenery of the wide Teesdale valley is to be found between Cross Fell where the River Tees rises, and Barnard Castle. Weardale provides fine walks over high moorland fells rising to more than 2000 feet. The Pennine Way loops through the western corner of Durham, starting with a stern 20-mile stretch with tough going between Tan Hill and Middleton-in-Teesdale.

Climbing Information

Dolerite outcrops of the high moorlands (e.g. High Cup Nick) tend not to offer worthwhile climbing. More amenable crags at lower altitudes:

1 Carboniferous limestone Two important developments are:

● **Windmore End** (823 167) over 1200 ft up on moorland edge 2 m. NE. of Brough holds some 90 climbs (usually harder) up to 40 ft.

● **Kings Meaburn** (618 213) in a pleasant setting beside R. Lyvennet opposite the village. A variety of steep climbs up to 45 ft.

2 Old red sandstone outcrops at several places in the Eden Valley: the following crags are very steep and offer fierce modern climbs of the highest standards:

● **Lazonby** (527 423) close to the river near the village some 6 m. NE. of Penrith has over 50 climbs (mostly very hard) up to 100 ft.

● **Armathwaite** (505 452) beside the Eden close to the village some 10 m. N. of Penrith offers over 50 climbs (mostly hard) up to 45 ft.

● **Scratchmere** (514 380) in a rural setting some 5 m. N. of Penrith holds over 20 climbs up to 45 ft.

Northumberland

Essential Information

Height: Average (including Cheviot Hills) between 1200 and 1800 ft; max. The Cheviot (2675 ft)
Area: North–south 54 miles; east–west 25 miles
Distances from main towns: Carlisle 13 miles; Penrith 19 miles; Newcastle 25 miles
Suggested bases: Hexham, Rothbury, Bellingham, Wooler

Access routes: A69 (south) between Hexham and Haltwhistle; A68 (central) between Otterburn and Carter Bar; B6410 and B6351 (north) between Wooler and Kirk Yetholm
BR stations: Haltwhistle, Hexham, Haydon Bridge
Youth hostels: Bellingham, Once Brewed, Acomb, Wooler, Byrness, Greenhead
OS maps: 74, 75, 80, 81, 86–8

In Northumberland, the North Pennines merge imperceptibly with the Cheviot Hills in a geological mixture of whinstone, granite, and sandstone.

At the heart of the county is the National Park which extends over 400 square miles; the Border Forest Park, to the west, covers a further 175 square

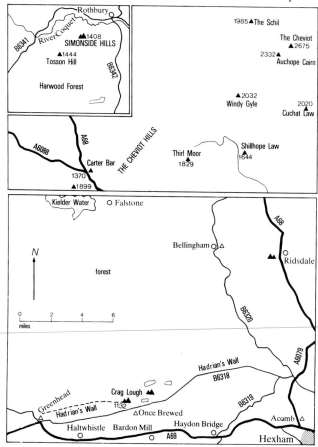

miles. More than two-thirds of Northumberland is hill country, of contrasting kinds; the granite mass of the Cheviot Hills in the western part are a series of round-topped, grass-covered individual summits, while the Simonside Hills in the east are more rugged, with sandstone outcrops pushing through a covering of heather.

The attractions of Northumberland lie in the diversity of its scenery, mirrored in the richness of the flora and fauna. The sternest section of the Pennine Way traverses the National Park for almost one-fifth of its total length. Finally, Northumberland has Hadrian's Wall.

The Pennine Way

The Pennine Way traces many of the remoter high spots. After entering from Cumbria it follows the line of Hadrian's Wall; the 8-mile section from Cawston is particularly memorable, following the bluff of Winshields Crag to Crag Lough. From Hadrian's Wall the path follows the boundary of the Border Forest, then turns to traverse the Cheviot range before it crosses into Scotland.

The Cheviot

At their highest point the Cheviot Hills rise to 2675 feet on the summit of The Cheviot. One ascent is via a path which branches off from the main Pennine Way, but there is easier access from Langleeford, south-west of Wooler. The Cheviot Hills are wild terrain which demand experience and respect from the walker.

Eastern Northumberland

Northumberland's second hill range, the Simonside Hills, offers more excellent walking to the south of Rothbury in Coquetdale. From the village, south-west of Alnwick, splendid way-marked tracks lead through the conifer forest that covers the northern slopes up to the main ridge. Here are nearly 10 miles of rugged heights, rising to their highest point on Tosson Hill (1444 feet). Upper Coquet Dale, where the Coquet rushes down from the Cheviots, is bounded by remote moorland which reaches 1829 feet on Thirl Moor.

Climbing Information

Many small outcrops of sandstone and gritstone, giving bouldering-type exercise.

1 Best-known crag is part of the **Whin Sill** formation – **quartz dolerite**:

● **Crag Lough** (768 678) north-facing cliff immediately below the Roman Wall some 4 m. NE. of Haltwhistle. Cliff is over 500 yds long and around 80 ft in height. Rock sound, smooth, and vertical standing as line of obelisk-like buttresses with steep bays between. Over 75 climbs, often of 2 pitch, tending towards easier grades. Popular cliff.
* 'Hadrians Wall': 50 ft. S.
* 'Great Chimney': 80 ft. S.
* 'Main Wall': 100 ft. S.

2 Most popular of the **sandstone** outcrops is:

● **Bowden Doors** (06 32) 4 m. NE. of Wooler. Nearly 100 ft high and some 200 yds long it holds over 50 climbs, generally of easier grades. Other similar sandstone outcrops have been developed:
● **Simonside** (02 98) 3 m. SW. of Rothbury.
● **Ravensheugh** (01 98) close by.
● **Great Whanney** (93 83) near Ridsdale.
● **Auchope Cairn** (891 200): several crags on the N. slopes of 2382-ft hill 1 m. SW. of The Cheviot. A dozen or so climbs in the easier grades up to 120 ft on intrusive **igneous** rock.

The Lammermuir and Moorfoot Hills

Essential Information

Height: Average between 1200 and 1650 ft; max. Blackhope Scar (Moorfoot Hills; 2137 ft)

Area: South-west to north-east 37 miles; north-west to south-east 14 miles

Distances from main towns: Berwick-upon-Tweed 15 miles; Edinburgh 17 miles

Suggested bases: Duns, Peebles

Access routes: A1 (east) between Berwick-upon-Tweed and Dunbar; A68 and A7 (central) between Melrose and Dalkeith; A72 (south-west) between Galashiels and Peebles

BR stations: Dunbar, Musselburgh

Youth hostels: Broadmeadows, Melrose

OS maps: 66, 67

The Southern Scottish Uplands stretch in a series of gently rounded hill ranges north from the Cheviots on the border with Northumberland to the edge of the central valley of the Clyde. This Borders region offers the walker a fine variety of routes over vast expanses of sweeping, heather-clad country, cut by glens, lochs, and rushing streams. Despite the proximity of Edinburgh to the north-west, there is still solitude to be found among these beautiful hills.

The Lammermuir Hills

The wide, wild slopes of the Lammermuir Hills rise to the south-east of Edinburgh, reaching 1755 feet at their highest point on Meikle Says Law. It is a lonely landscape given over mainly to sheep-farming, with only few scattered villages. On their eastern side the hills are bounded by a fine stretch of coast which gives some exhilarating walking, particularly between St Abb's Head and Dunbar.

The charming little town of Duns, north of Coldstream, is a good base from which to explore the Lammermuirs. One particularly splendid route winds northward for 14 miles along a hill path, with a few short road sections, to Cockburnspath on the coast. On its way it passes the lovely Whiteadder Water set in the main river valley which cuts through the hills. To the west lie Longformacus and the Watch Water reservoir, another worthwhile objective. Well-defined tracks link the two waters, and further paths run down to Lauderdale

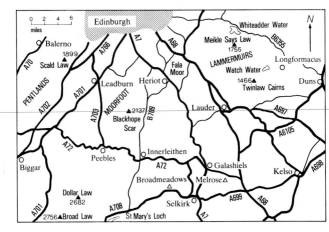

to the south, skirting Twinlaw Cairns (1466 feet).

The Whiteadder Water set in the midst of the Lammermuir Hills.

The Moorfoot Hills

The Moorfoot Hills extend in a short curve to the west of the Lammermuirs, separated by Fala Moor; at their highest point on Blackhope Scar they rise to 2137 feet. The Moorfoots offer yet more exhilarating, and varied, high-level walking. From Peebles a 12-mile route leads along tracks and forestry roads to Leithen Water. This is an interesting and easy path, rising gently to over 1700 feet and then descending to Craighope. The walk can be extended to Innerleithen, some 6 miles to the south.

Along the southern flank of the Moorfoot Hills lies Glentress Forest, the first to be established in Southern Scotland by the Forestry Commission. Now covering nearly 2500 acres, it provides a blend of woodland and hill walking over a choice of tracks and paths. The access point is 2 miles east of Peebles, off the A72. For sterner, and grander, terrain, take the upland track from Leadburn (north of Peebles on the A703) to Heriot. A fine col route and ancient trackway lead via Mauldslie Hill, open moor, and Tathieknowe Burn to Heriot Water, a distance of 17 miles.

South of Peebles lie the beauty spots of St Mary's Loch and Megget Water. From here there is a choice of paths, including the easy route to the summit of Broad Law to the north-west, at 2756 feet the second highest hill in Southern Scotland.

The Pentland Hills

On the south-western doorstep of Edinburgh lie the gentle Pentland Hills, rising in a series of individual peaks. Numerous paths cross the hills, starting from the two main roads that enclose them to north and south. One fine 9-mile route runs from Balerno on the A70 to Penicuik, crossing Scald Law (1899 feet).

The Ochil Hills

Essential Information

Height: Average between 1300 and
2000 ft; max. Ben Cleuch (2364 ft)
Area: South-west to north-east 23 miles;
north-west to south-east 8 miles
Distances from main towns: Stirling
3 miles; Perth 8 miles; Edinburgh
25 miles
Suggested bases: Glendevon, Dunblane
Access routes: A9 (north) between
Bridge of Allan and Perth; A91 (south)
between Stirling and Milnathort; A823
(central) between Gleneagles Station
and Yetts of Muckhart
BR stations: Gleneagles, Dunblane
Youth hostels: Stirling, Glendevon,
Perth, Falkland
OS map: 58

North of the Firth of Forth
lie more gentle and pretty
stretches of upland terrain. The
Ochils rise handsomely north-
east of Stirling and extend
almost to the outskirts of Perth.
The grass-covered hills are cut
by many glens and waters. One
of the recognized distance
routes in these hills which
attracts walkers traverses the
range south-west to north-east,
via tracks and minor roads,
using youth hostels as overnight stops.

The most rugged terrain,
and the most isolated with the
least number of roads, lies to

the west of Gleneagles. Here
rise Ben Cleuch (2364 feet),
and King's Seat Hill near Castle
Campbell, reaching 2126 feet.
There is gentler walking towards Perth, following lanes
and tracks, with pretty hill
country being revealed from
the Path of Condie along the
Water of May.

It is the central range that
holds the most appeal for
lovers of high country, where
Glen Eagles and Glen Devon
form a regal pass, flanked by a
host of lesser braes. The whole
area is now an acknowledged
outdoor leisure ground shared
by the Central and Tayside
regions. The village of Glendevon is a popular base with
hill-walkers who have superb
country in almost every direction, with a distinct flavour of
the true Highlands further to
the north.

The Lomond Hills

To the south-west of Falkland
on the eastern side of Loch
Leven rise the Lomond Hills.
From Falkland, which is
reached via Auchtermuchty off
the A91, tracks lead to the top
of West Lomond (1713 feet),
the main summit, around quiet

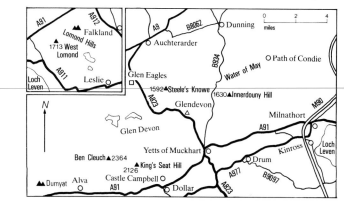

The Ochil Hills: (above) near Bridge of Allan, (below) from Vane Hill.

reservoirs, the haunt of deer and seabirds. The whole range is crossed by many footpaths. From the summit heights there are splendid views in all directions, even reaching to the Cairngorms in clear conditions.

Climbing Information

No inland cliffs of importance although several outcrops are steep enough to have been climbed on. The two most developed are:

1 Ochils: 'The Great Glen' (835 975) is an open gully between the main and W. tops of Dumyat hill. There are several climbs up to 50 ft or so on friable **volcanic breccia** or 'puddingstone' (most in the easier grades). 2 m. E. of Bridge of Allan.

2 Lomonds: Craigengaw (210 082) lies on the plateau rim just NE. of summit of West Lomond, some 6 m. NE. of Kinross. Several climbs (mostly in easier grades), but up to 130 ft max. on vegetatious **dolerite**.

The Lowther Hills to Glen Trool

Essential Information

Height: Average between 1300 and 2000 ft; max. The Merrick (2766 ft)
Area: North-east to south-west 55 miles; north-west to south-east 15 miles
Distances from main towns: Ayr 10 miles; Dumfries 10 miles; Carlisle 35 miles
Suggested bases: Moffat, Newton Stewart
Access routes: A714 (west) between Newton Stewart and Barrhill; A76 (central) between Dumfries and New Cumnock; A74 (east) between Lockerbie and Crawford
BR stations: Lockerbie, Dumfries
Youth hostels: Wanlockhead, Glenhoul
OS maps: 78, 79, 84

The Southern Scottish Uplands do not exceed 2800 feet at any point, and there are few of the corries, sharp ridges, or steep buttresses that are so characteristic of the Highland ranges. Moffat, on the eastern fringe of the Borders region, is an excellent centre for hill-walkers. Three lengthy paths start from the town: to Tushielaw Inn, 20 miles north-east via Ettrick Water; to Tweedsmuir, 16 miles north via Fruid reservoir;

and a third northwards to Crawford, largely along a Roman road, skirting the Devil's Beef Tub, then crossing a wide forestry plantation.

The Lowther Hills

The Lowther Hills rise to the west of Moffat, their twin ranges forming a V-shape enclosing the Daer reservoir. These secluded hills, covered with grass and heather, offer invigorating walking on a variety of good footpaths.

An exhilarating walk across the central range follows the old railway track from Elvanfoot, 2 miles south of Crawford, alongside Elvan Water westwards to Leadhills. From here a marked path ascends to Wanlockhead, skirting west and south of Green Lowther (2403 feet), the highest point in the range. The two villages of Leadhills and Wanlockhead are the highest in Scotland, at over 1300 feet. From Green Lowther the route then largely follows Enterkin Burn down to Nithsdale and Carron bridge at the junction of the A76 and

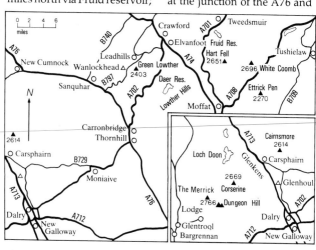

A702 some 15 miles away.

Glen Trool

Arguably the most beautiful corner of Dumfries & Galloway in the south-west of Scotland is around Loch Trool. Here rise a cluster of remote granite peaks, in grandeur reminiscent of the Highlands, set within the wide Galloway Forest Park. From the Forestry centre and camp ground (itself remote and far removed from the tourist traffic) a splendid hill-track ascends for nearly 5 miles to the summit of The Merrick (2766 feet), the highest in Southern Scotland. The reward is a panoramic view over Loch Enoch, one of a string of waters, glittering a thousand feet below. This is only one of several short walks in the area.

For long-distance walkers there is a glorious 25-mile trek from Bargrennan north-east

Glen Trool.

right across the Park to Carsphairn on the A713 in the Glenkens. En route lie the Rhinns of Kells, reaching 2669 feet on the peak of Corserine. The most direct ascent and the quickest access to the Rhinns ridge is via the minor road off the A713, 2 miles north of Dalry. From Polharrow Burn a track leads at first through forest and then over North Gairy Top to Corserine in its grand and isolated setting.

Climbing Information

Although there are outcrops of a wide variety of different rocks scattered throughout the Southern Uplands and Central Lowlands, there are no important climbing cliffs although some climbs have been made on most. Several of the better cliffs include:

● **Kirkennan Crag** (822 579): 2 m. SW. of Dalbeattie close to A711. Several climbs on a small but superb **granite** buttress rising from woods in an attractive situation.

● **Clifton Crags** (909 572): 6 m. SE. of Dalbeattie close to the Solway shore. A line of **granite** cliffs (probably once actually sea-cliffs) give 20 or 30 routes up to 80 ft (all grades), most of them easier standard.

● **Dungeon Hill** (462 849): Cooran Buttress offers a 350-ft VD. route on good **granite** on the E. face of this hill (2020 ft)

overlooking the Cooran Valley some 2 m. SE. of Merrick.

● **Loudoun Hill** (609 379): an ancient **volcanic plug** rising to 1036 ft amid rolling rural country 3 m. E. of Darvel and clearly visible just N. of A71. S. and E. faces offer a dozen good climbs and many variations up to 200 ft in length (mostly VD and S).

● **Traprain Law** (582 747): 3 m. E. of Haddington. Over 70 recorded climbs on two popular S.-facing crags on steep slabs of **trachyte** (igneous rock). Routes are of every grade and up to 200 ft in length.

● **Salisbury Crags:** on slopes of Arthur's Seat in Queen's Park, Edinburgh. These basalt crags offer several hundred routes of all standards and up to 100 ft in length. But they lie within the city boundaries and access is officially discouraged.

Downland

The word 'down' derives from the Old English *dune*, or hill, especially the smooth-contoured kind bare of trees. In Britain these rounded uplands are essentially a feature of the south-east, cropped by sheep for centuries, now mainly arable land or conservation areas.

Although broken up into distinctive groups, the downlands all spring geologically from the great chalk table centred on Dorset, Wiltshire, and Hampshire. From here long chalk spines span southern England, creating what is known collectively as the Western Downs. The spread of chalk from Wessex is very extensive, running north-east in a widening belt to the Norfolk coast and south-east in two major spurs to form the North and South Downs.

For walkers – especially those discovering, or rediscovering, that walking is not so much work as sheer enjoyment – the downs provide near-perfect terrain. Here the novice may graduate to a more experienced grade

1 The Dorset Downs
2 The North Wessex Downs
3 The Hampshire Downs
4 The North Downs
5 The South Downs

safely and not too strenuously. Countryside and climate are both benign; the pedestrian traveller is never more than a short distance from civilization (apart perhaps from odd pockets of Dorset or Wiltshire), and most of the downland ridges are within easy reach of the great south-eastern conurbations.

The biggest single advantage for the newcomer to hill-walking, however, is the wealth of established long-distance downland footpaths. Now way-marked, much walked, and easily identifiable for the most part, these tracks wind invitingly along or just below the crests of all the major chalk heights, from South Foreland in Kent to western Dorset above Portland Bill.

Indeed, it would scarcely be possible to recommend two more appropriate introductions to distance-walking than the South Downs Way or the Berkshire/Wiltshire section of the Ridgeway.

Practical points

● Chalk tracks, particularly those which are much walked and peppered with protruding flints, are hard on the feet during long, dry spells. Even though contours are relatively gentle do not be too ambitious when planning your daily distance: 12 miles is a reasonable target for beginners carrying a pack.

● In wet weather, chalk surfaces can be slippery and sometimes deceptively treacherous on sharp inclines. Always wear proper hill-walking boots with non-slip soles, and oversocks to cushion the feet.

● Many downland long-distance paths are also bridleways in part, permitting cyclists and horse-riders the same right of way as walkers. Horses can turn low-lying sections into quagmires after prolonged rain. It is usually possible to avoid the worst by picking your way, but it is also tedious and time-consuming. Allow for such hold-ups and carry dry socks in your pack. At the end of the day they may be badly needed.

● All the downland areas are heavily populated by visitors in summer (and increasingly at week-ends throughout the year). Regrettably, it is becoming risky to leave your car at the starting-points of footpaths, even locked and empty of valuables. Choose your car-parking spot with prudence: a local pub or in the vicinity of a police station (preferably with prior notice) is safer.

● Because of sheer numbers, it is sensible, not to say almost obligatory now, to make prior overnight arrangements along all recognized downland routes. This is essential in high summer to avoid annoyance and inconvenience.

● Lightweight camping – back-packing – obviates much, if not all, such anxiety. It also adds a new dimension of independence and self-reliance. Make sure the back-pack load is lightweight, however, and always seek permission before pitching for the night.

DOWNLAND

The Dorset Downs

Essential Information

Height: Average between 500 and 750 ft; max. Pilsden Pen (909 ft)
Area: North–south 8 miles; east–west 26 miles
Distances from main towns: Dorchester 3 miles; Yeovil 6 miles; Bournemouth 15 miles
Suggested bases: Dorchester, Beaminster
Access routes: A356 (south and west) between Dorchester and Crewkerne; A352 (central) between Sherborne and Dorchester; A357 (east) between Blandford Forum and Sherborne
BR stations: Dorchester, Maiden Newton, Yeovil Junction
Youth hostels: Bridport, Litton Cheney
OS maps: 193,194

The main upland sweep of the Dorset Downs runs in a broad arc from east to west above Dorchester, stretching from Blandford Forum to Beaminster, between Blackmoor Vale and the sea. Although rarely rising above 800 feet, the chalk ridge affords exhilarating views: northwards over the lush Blackmoor Vale, southwards towards the coast and Isle of Portland, west to Eggardon Hill.

In contrast to the friendly aspect of the green downs stands the gorse and heather wilderness of the Dorset Heath which extends to the east of the chalk ridge. Narrow and secluded valleys cut by streams and springs run through the downland. There is almost an embarrassment of scenic riches littering the Dorset Downs, from earliest prehistoric times up to recent centuries. Although crowded with visitors in the summer, there are footpaths and seclusion in abundance for those who are prepared to wander away from the mainstream of traffic.

The ancient hunting ground of Cranborne Chase, from Charlton Down.

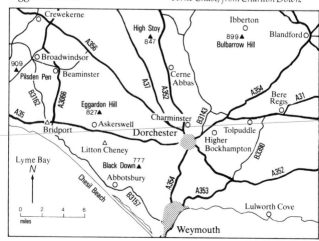

The northern ridge

It is the heights around Ibberton, west of Blandford Forum, that reward the walker with the widest panoramas. Several delightful high-level routes start from Ibberton: along signposted bridleways to Okeford Hill, or to the summit of Bulbarrow Hill (899 feet) further south-west, crowned by an Iron Age earthworks.

Historic tracks and landmarks

Of the many ancient landmarks which punctuate the Dorset Downs the most exciting is Maiden Castle, the largest Iron Age earthworks in Europe, which dates back more than 2000 years. It is located a little off the main downland ridge, 2 miles south-west of Dorchester. The site extends over some 125 acres, forming a fascinating series of intricate contours; to see it properly takes half a day.

Further west, beyond Dorchester and north of Askerswell on the A35, lies Eggardon hillfort, considered to be one of the most striking in Wessex. There are fine views extending from the summit of the hill (827 feet) which can be reached by a variety of routes.

More evidence of early man is revealed by the prehistoric hill-track which begins alongside the B3143, 2 miles north-east of Dorchester, and leads to Charminster along a chalk ridge strewn with burial mounds. The landscape hereabouts still retains a delightful air of pastoral England, reflected in the names of many of the villages. Ancient mystery of a different kind surrounds the Cerne Abbas Giant, cut from the chalk hillside above the village of Cerne Abbas. The

Gently undulating landscape near Bridport, in the south of the county.

vast figure, a legendary fertility symbol, wields a huge club and is of Roman or earlier origins. There is fine hill-walking from the village north-west to High Stoy Hill.

The conspicuous landmark of Badbury Rings Iron Age hill-fort can be reached via the B3082 approach road to Blandford Forum from Wimborne. There is a fascinating walk which runs round the massive, tree-cloaked summit.

Two monuments to more recent history also offer attractive walking. The first is the monument to Admiral Hardy set on the 777-foot summit of Black Down, inland from Abbotsbury on a loop of the South-West Peninsula Path; there are some ten Bronze Age burial mounds in the vicinity. The second is Thomas Hardy's cottage at Higher Bockhampton, 4 miles from Dorchester. A number of paths run through the area, to the seclusion of Beacon Hill or through Thorncombe Wood.

Pilsden Pen, the highest point at 909 feet, is a fine heather-clad chalk hill, topped by an ancient earthwork and reached via an easy path from the B3164, south-west of Broadwindsor. From the summit there are splendid views over Marshwood Vale unfolding to the south.

The North Wessex Downs

Essential Information

Height: Average between 650 and 850 ft; max. Tan Hill (964 ft)
Area: North-east to south-west 38 miles; north-west to south-east 10 miles
Distances from main towns: Swindon 4 miles; Reading 10 miles; Oxford 13 miles
Suggested bases: Devizes, Marlborough, Wantage
Access routes: A34 (east) between Newbury and Harwell; A338 (central) between Hungerford and Wantage; M4 (central), exits 13, 14, and 15; A361 (west) between Devizes and Swindon
BR stations: Hungerford, Pewsey, Goring-on-Thames, Didcot, Swindon
Youth hostels: Upper Inglesham, Streatley-on-Thames
OS maps: 164, 173, 174, 175, 183, 184

This chalk downland swathe, known variously as the Berkshire or Wiltshire Downs, and in some parts along its length as the Lambourn or Marlborough Downs, collectively forms the North Wessex Downs. This unique upland region contains more signs of prehistoric civilization than almost anywhere else in the British Isles. With a green and beautiful landscape which is still gloriously – and miraculously – bypassed in the main by modern development, and an easy way-marked track which traces the entire crestline, the whole area becomes an objective to fire the enthusiasm of every leisure-walker.

The green and rounded summits of the Berkshire Downs extend for some 25 miles to the west of the Chilterns from Goring Gap, before veering southwards into Wiltshire as the Marlborough Downs. These Wessex Downs have been important for both arable and sheep farming since the late Stone Age and agriculture still plays a large part today.

The Ridgeway Path

It is possible to follow this prehistoric track for 43 miles from Goring-on-Thames along the crest of the Downs to Overton Hill. West of Streatley-on-Thames, where the ancient Great Ridgeway succeeds the equally ancient Icknield Way, the bridleway crosses Roden Downs and the battlefield site of Ashdown, where Alfred the Great vanquished the Danes in the ninth century. Much earlier and absorbing relics litter this hill route: Grim's Ditch, Segsbury Camp, and Uffington Castle. Near by is the most elegant – and enigmatic – chalk-cut horse in Europe on Whitehorse Hill, conceivably Iron Age, though perhaps much earlier. The landscape

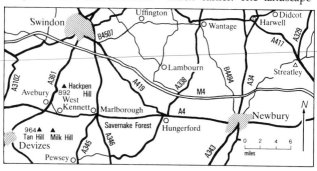

68

Cherhill Down, from Yatesbury Field. The Cherhill White Horse, from the west.

flat-topped dome. Much speculation and mystery surround the mound, the largest man-made hill in Western Europe, constructed around 2500 BC. To appreciate the maximum atmosphere, this route is best walked during the week or out of season.

Vale of Pewsey

The Wessex Downs rise to their highest point above the Vale of Pewsey, west of Savernake Forest, between Marlborough and Devizes, reaching 964 feet on the summit of Tan Hill. Along the crest of the ridge of hills runs the Wansdyke, an ancient boundary line or fortification, thought to date from the fifth century. The original 25-foot-high bank can still be seen in places. The Ridgeway meets the Wansdyke below Milk Hill, immediately east of Tan Hill. To the north-west the high ground runs out at Cherhill Down (853 ft), graced by another but less ancient White Horse, above the A4 Bath road, close to Calne.

around Whitehorse Hill is also beautifully dramatic, while the immaculately preserved neolithic burial chamber of Wayland's Smithy in its haunting setting a little further west makes a lasting impact on most walkers.

Further riches await the walker approaching from the north-east. Beyond Barbury Castle on its 850-foot vantage point and Hackpen Hill (892 feet) via an avenue of sarsen stones lie the great long barrow of West Kennett, and the majestic Avebury Stone Circle. About one mile west of Avebury, alongside the A4, is Silbury Hill, rising 130 feet in a

The Hampshire Downs

Essential Information

Height: Average between 450 and 750 ft; max. Walbury Hill (974 ft)

Area: North-west to south 38 miles; south-west to north-east 10 miles

Distances from main towns: Basingstoke 5 miles; Portsmouth 8 miles; Southampton 9 miles; Newbury 6 miles

Suggested bases: Petersfield, Winchester, Romsey

Access routes: A343 (north) between Andover and Newbury; A339 (north) between Alton and Newbury; A31 (central) between Farnham and Winchester; A272 (south) between Winchester and Petersfield.

BR stations: Alton, Andover, Basingstoke, Alresford, Winchester, Petersfield, Hungerford, etc.

Youth hostels: Winchester, Overton, Southampton, Portsmouth

OS maps: 185, 186, 196, 197

The magnet of Hampshire for the majority of visitors is the New Forest, which leaves some gentle, delightful down-land that much freer of summer crowds, and minor access roads less choked with traffic. The half-moon of the Hampshire Downs starts in the north-west corner of the county (north of Andover) and curves south and east in a wide swathe to the Sussex border above Chichester harbour. The uplands are formed by the declining western limits of the North and South Downs, both of which link and blend within Hampshire's boundaries as they approach the uplands of Salisbury Plain.

There is still enough height in those western fringes to provide 900 feet of elevation on some crests. The hills around Alton are the joining line of the North and South Downs, although the former also run north-west of Basingstoke to

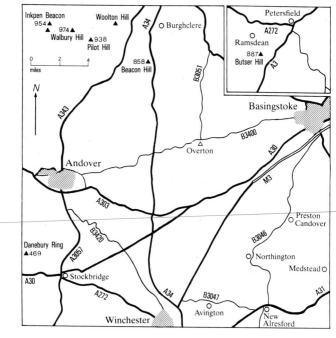

Inkpen Hill. View from the north-west over the village of Shalbourne.

the Berkshire border. The South Downs decline at a lower height generally via Winchester and towards Salisbury Plain, but they do boast Pilot Hill (938 feet), Hampshire's highest.

Northern Hampshire

The charm of old Hampshire can be found in numerous downland pockets, despite massive urbanization of the county since World War II. The area around Alresford, split into Old and New by the River Aire, is one example. From here there is pleasant walking to Northington and Medstead over tracks and lanes, also to Avington with its pretty cluster of riverside cottages.

North-east of Alresford there is more quiet country walking, notably over stretches of the Droveway, an ancient track in the vicinity of Preston Candover, reached via the B3046.

North-west of Basingstoke from the historic village of Burghclere there is an impressive footpath ascent of Beacon Hill topped by an Iron Age camp, with panoramas from nearly 860 feet. Just west of Burghclere there is the National Trust nature reserve at Woolton Hill, close to the Berkshire border. Westwards from Beacon Hill the scarp continues to the highest point at the

Iron Age camp at Walbury Hill (974 feet), Combe Gibbet, and Inkpen Beacon (954 feet), all actually just in Berkshire. The view from the airy turf encompasses the Kennet Valley.

On the north-eastern county boundary there is more beautiful hilly terrain, especially north-west of Farnham in the area around Crondall village, which is richly endowed with ancient relics; Caesar's Camp earthworks and a section of the prehistoric Harrow Way are two of them. The vicinity of Stockbridge in the west offers a variety of hill walks largely over National Trust terrain, especially just to the east where the chalk downs are littered with Iron Age relics, including Woodbury Camp hill-fort.

Butser Hill

Butser Hill, some 3 miles southwest of Petersfield, marks another high point of the Hampshire Downs, rising to 887 feet. From the gorse-clad summit there are splendid views over Portsmouth and the Solent as far as the Isle of Wight. Both Butser Hill and the nearby Ramsdean Down are ancient barrows. This area is now designated as the Queen Elizabeth Country Park.

DOWNLAND

The North Downs

Essential Information

Height: Average between 450 and 650 ft; max. Leith Hill (965 ft)
Area: West to south-east 90 miles; breadth ¾ mile
Distances from main towns: Central London to Dorking 22 miles; Central London to Maidstone 33 miles
Suggested bases: Dorking, Guildford, Maidstone
Access routes: A31 (west) between Farnham and Guildford; A25 (central) between Guildford and Maidstone; A20 (south-east) between Maidstone and Dover
BR stations: Farnham, Reigate, Sevenoaks, Maidstone, Ashford, Folkestone, Dover, etc.
Youth hostels: Tanners Hatch, Holmbury St Mary, Crockham Hill, Kemsing, Dover
OS maps: 179, 185, 186, 187, 188, 189

The chalk line of the North Downs extends for nearly 100 miles, allowing for the natural breaches and overlays of later, sedimentary rocks which date from the Cretaceous Period of somewhere between 70 and 130 million years ago. The longest chalk ridge in Britain, the North Downs rise in Hampshire and continue to South Foreland, finishing as the White Cliffs of Dover. Paths cross the Downs in all directions, and the North Downs Way effectively traverses all the beauty areas between Farnham and the coast. The North Downs offer many opportunities for the leisure walker which are all within easy reach of London, with extensive views stretching over farming country to the north and over the Kentish Weald to the south.

The North Downs Way

The North Downs Way follows an ancient track for 140 miles along the ridge of the North Downs, keeping as close to the summit as possible. The long-distance path passes very close to the London suburbs and the Medway conurbation; route-finding is difficult in places; there is a certain amount of road-walking (especially along the western half); and some parts are distinctly overgrown. None the less, there is pretty countryside in between, with one or two pockets that are memorable, and the route does take the walker through a swathe of England steeped in every age of history. Walking conditions throughout the long-distance path are good, along paths and quiet lanes, though some stretches do become overgrown in summer.

The Hog's Back, rising to 500 feet and more amid lush wooded slopes between Farnham and Guildford, is one impressive point. Here some 12 miles of the Pilgrim's Way run below its southern slopes to Guildford. To the east of the ancient county town are the charming delights of Shere, Gomshall, Abinger Hanger. There is good walking over Hackhurst Downs and around Shere and the Silent Pool.

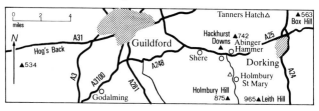

Near Otford, north of Sevenoaks.

Leith Hill

The North Downs rise to their highest point on the summit of Leith Hill (965 feet), the culminating point of the greensand ridge which parallels the chalk ridge between Guildford and Dorking, a few miles to its south. In clear conditions the view from the 64-foot tower that crowns the hill extends over the Weald and the Downs beyond as far as the Kentish hills and the Channel. There are equally magnificent vistas from Holmbury Hill (875 feet), to the west of Leith Hill. The whole area provides excellent walking. An 8-acre Iron Age hill-fort lies on the slopes around Holmbury Hill.

There is further good walking over the 472 acres of Ranmore Common (National Trust) which lies on a ridge of the Downs below the western slopes of Box Hill, 2 miles north-west of Dorking. A variety of footpaths, some of them way-marked, run through beautiful woods of beech and oak. From the steep slopes which ascend to the Common there are wide views south towards the Kentish Weald.

Box Hill area

The scenery around the well-known beauty spot of Box Hill, protected by the National Trust, is as fine as any in southern England. There are splendid views westwards from the 560-foot summit which is crossed by many footpaths. The long-distance path climbs Box Hill, continuing eastwards across Brockham and Betchworth Hills, cloaked with the box-trees that give Box Hill its name. Colley Hill, above a great chalk scarp, is another impressive viewpoint; from here, the path runs on to Reigate Hill.

Eastwards, relatively unspoilt country starts again above Oxted with the Chevening estate – containing the famous 'keyhole' viewpoint – and both flanks of the pretty Darent Valley as worthy of special mention. Hereabouts the greensand ridge again rises to the south around Chartwell and Ide Hill and Knole Park. The steep escarpment, crowned with fine woods and giving wide panoramas across the Eden Valley to Ashdown Forest, rises to 771 feet at The Chart, above Brasted.

Now the Downs lose height and fade into the depths of east Kent. Wye Downs (583 feet), north-east of Ashford, offer steep slopes and attractive walking beside the Broad Downs nature reserve. Finally, shapely hills occur again behind Folkestone, where Tolsford Hill reaches 594 feet.

The South Downs

Essential Information

Height: Average between 500 and 700 ft; max. Graffham Down (836 ft)
Area: East–west 56 miles; north–south 7 miles
Distances from main towns: Brighton 3 miles; Portsmouth 8 miles
Suggested bases: Brighton, Bognor Regis, Chichester
Access routes: A286 (west) between Chichester and Midhurst; A24 (central) between Worthing and Washington; A23 (central) between Brighton and Pycombe; A22 (east) between Eastbourne and Polegate
BR stations: Eastbourne, Lewes, Brighton, Arundel, Chichester, etc.
Youth hostels: Arundel, Patcham, Alfriston, Beachy Head, Telscombe, Truleigh Hill
OS maps: 197, 198, 199

Unlike the North Downs, the South Downs are compact, and contained almost within one county. Few points rise above 800 feet, but the chalk ridge is nevertheless majestic, culminating in the most dramatic high spot on the southern English coast, Beachy Head, which rises for 534 feet sheer from the waters of the English Channel.

The well-defined route of the South Downs Way follows the ridge of the Downs, within sight of the sea for almost all its length. In addition, there are numerous footpaths and tracks, many of ancient origin, which crisscross the Downs, providing easy and practical walking at every season of the year.

The South Downs Way

This 80-mile long-distance path, the easiest and one of the most enjoyable in Britain, traverses East and West Sussex from Eastbourne to Buriton near Petersfield, just over the Hampshire border. There are two possible routes from the start of the Way, one inland and one which follows the coast. This second route crosses the cliffs of Beachy Head and continues westwards to the chalk cliffs of the Seven Sisters. Beyond Birling Gap the path descends to Cuckmere Haven, then turns north to join the inland bridleway route from Eastbourne.

This loop path is no less intriguing, since some of the finest views along the South Downs await the walker who climbs Windover Hill. On the northern slope is the celebrated chalk-cut figure of Wilmington Long Man, dominating the village below. The two routes join at Alfriston and continue west, skirting Firle Beacon, at 713 feet the highest point of the eastern South Downs.

Above the bustle of Brighton, the Downs remain detached, unspoiled, and quietly beautiful alongside the long-distance path. Particularly notable is the stretch between Ditchling Beacon (813 feet) and Devil's Dyke, a massive and regal

View westwards from Devil's Dyke.

combe. Truly wonderful views extend from the summit of the Beacon over the surrounding downland. Beyond the River Adur, north of Worthing, lies Chanctonbury Ring, its wind-swept summit (779 feet) dominating the skyline for miles around. The remains of an Iron Age fort crown the hill, containing a grove of beech-trees within its circle.

West Sussex

West of Harrow Hill, beyond the river Arun, lies the pride of the West Sussex high country, above Goodwood and Chichester. The South Downs rise to their highest point on Graffham Down (836 feet), north-east of Chichester between the hamlets of Houghton and Cocking. The area is rich in ancient landmarks: the line of the Roman Stane Street, once linking Chichester with London and Colchester, which crosses the Downs on the summit of Bignor Hill (737 feet), and the Roman villa at Bignor, one of the largest in Britain, containing beautiful mosaic floors.

There is another fine view-point on Beacon Hill (793 feet) above Harting Downs. The ascent to the summit, defined by the ramparts of an Iron Age hill-fort, gives increasingly wide views, north to the Weald and south over the Channel. The South Downs Way skirts the south of Beacon Hill on its route east towards Buriton.

Climbing Information

In Tunbridge Wells area, midway between North and South Downs, a core of **cretaceous sand** forms the Forest Ridge. Several small outcrops appear, some large enough to provide short climbs of bouldering type, important only because of their proximity to London and consequent popularity. Rock is soft and friable and never more than 45 ft high. When dry, offers friction akin to gritstone, forms deep cracks and chimneys and rounded bulging overhangs. Best known craglets are:
● **Harrison's Rocks** (532 354): 1 m. S. of Groombridge. Owned by B.M.C./Sports Council. Some 600 yds of 'edge' holding over 150 recorded climbs (all grades).
● **High Rocks** (560 382): 1½ m. W. of Tunbridge Wells. Over 100 climbs, few actually easy.
● **Bowles Rocks** (543 330): 2½ m. S. of Groombridge. Many excellent climbs. Operated as a commercial 'klettergarten' and outdoor pursuits centre.

Mountains

The mountain ranges of Britain are the result of convulsions of the earth's cooling crust, anything from 450 million to 4500 million years ago. Geologically speaking, the volcanic peaks of the Lake District are 'young', while the Cambrians and the Torridonian peaks are 'old'. A simplistic definition certainly, since the variety and mixture of rock formations make the British Isles as complex and fascinating as any in the world.

Yet while the mountains are exciting and deeply rewarding for the walker, they are by the same token dangerous if not respected. Over 200 people die each year among the British mountains. Newcomers should hasten slowly and, if they wish to progress to rock-climbing, should not neglect to become safe and proficient hill-walkers: many climbing crags are located in the innermost recesses of the mountains. Conversely, hill-walkers should be able to cope with 'scrambling': negotiating rocky terrain where hands as

1 The Brecon Beacons National Park
2 The Cambrian Mountains
3 The Cumbrian Mountains
4 Snowdonia
5 Queen Elizabeth Forest Park and the Trossachs
6 The Southern and Central Highlands
7 The Monadhliath Mountains
8 The Cairngorms
9 Glen Nevis and Glen Coe
10 Glen Cannich, Glen Affric, Glen Shiel
11 The Torridons and Wester Ross
12 The Northern Highlands

well as feet must be used, but which is not sufficiently awkward to necessitate the rock-climber's rope and techniques.

Weather in our mountains can change swiftly and dramatically and, especially in the winter months, what started as a pleasant hike can end as a battle for survival. Winter must be taken seriously. Snow and ice can render easy ridges, slopes, and even paths extremely dangerous to the inexperienced or ill-equipped. Snow avalanches do happen even among the most gentle-seeming hills and they claim victims every year after heavy snowfalls or during the thaw.

It is not necessary, however, to storm every summit in order to enjoy the mountains. For many enthusiasts it is reward enough simply to be among the mountains, absorbing their grandeur from valley floor or hill-tracks on the lower slopes. If a peak does exert an irresistible pull, ensure conditions are favourable and temper over-eager ambition with prudence.

Practical Points

● Training is important. Get used to walking, even in the city and on the way to work. Eschew the lift and take the stairs! Basic mountain skills – and more – can be learnt and practised at Outdoor Centres and on courses or with clubs throughout the country.

● Walking from a set base is an excellent ploy in the early stages. The longer the stay, the more local knowledge will be absorbed, especially for the novice staying at a recognized Outdoor Centre, where expert advice and guided walks or climbs will be available.

● Longer itineraries should always be carefully planned, with the emphasis on proficiency and safety. Parties of three or four people are preferable. Walk at the pace of the slowest, avoid stringing out, especially in deteriorating weather conditions. Make sure at least one person is properly proficient with map and compass. Work out on the map escape routes from the high ground should the weather turn too fierce to proceed.

● Backpackers have an advantage in that they literally carry their home with them. With the right amount and weight of equipment they can camp for days at a time if need be. Such self-reliance increases confidence and scope.

● Be prepared (and equipped) for emergencies. Know the standard distress signal: six whistle-blasts or torch-flashes per minute. Carry spare clothing, both weather-proofs and warmers. Remember even a 10 mph breeze will drop a still-air temperature of 4°F to freezing-point! Carry quick-energy foods such as chocolate and mint-cake or glucose; a hot drink, or the light-weight means to make it, can be a real morale-booster in emergency. But do not overdo what you carry – an extra 20 lb of emergency gear may mean the difference between having to use it or not. Listen to weather forecasts, understand weather signs, and learn to recognize and treat hypothermia or 'exposure' symptoms. Know something of basic first aid.

The Brecon Beacons National Park

Essential Information

Height: Average between 1750 and 2100 ft; max. Pen y Fan (2906 ft)

Area: North-east to south-west 48 miles; north-west to south-east 15 miles

Distances from main towns: Merthyr Tydfil 3 miles; Hereford 10 miles; Swansea 13 miles; Cardiff 23 miles

Suggested bases: Brecon, Llandovery, Abergavenny, Crickhowell

Access routes: A479 (north-east) between Tretower and Talgarth; B4423 (north-east) between Llanfihangel Crucorney and Hay-on-Wye; A40 (central) between Crickhowell and Llandovery; A4069 (south-west) between Pontardawe and Llandovery

BR stations: Llandovery, Abergavenny, Merthyr Tydfil

Youth hostels: Ystradfellte, Llwyn-y-Celyn, Capel-y-Ffin, Llanddeusant, Ty'n-y-Caeau, Crickhowell

OS maps: 160, 161, 171

The spectacular crests of the Brecon Beacons, composed of Devonian Sandstone some 350 million years old, dominate the landscape of South Wales. Together with the Black Mountain to the west and the Black Mountains to the east, they make up the Brecon Beacons National Park. It is a wild landscape of many faces: peaks and ridges rising above bracken-clad moors, limestone crags cut by steep wooded valleys and rushing streams, vast tracts of common land flanked by more pastoral, farming country. The area is dotted with lakes, including the placid Llangorse, and is divided by the fertile Usk Valley which lies between the Brecons and the Black Mountains.

The whole National Park comprises a natural leisure area containing a wealth of attractions. Climbers and hill-walkers have over 500 square miles to roam. For students of wildlife and history there are three nature reserves, and Llangorse Lake is rich in bird life. The excavated fortress settlement at Y Gaer near Brecon and Sarn Helen hill-track are just two Roman landmarks of distinction.

The limestone area contains the longest known cave system in Britain (over 12 miles), including Agen Allwedd near Brecon and the more accessible caverns at Dan yr Ogof. There is also the quietly scenic

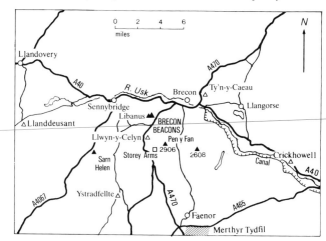

Brecons, above Cwm Oergwm.

Brecon-Abergavenny Canal (now a leisure waterway), which winds for over 30 miles from Brecon to Pontypool, for those who prefer gentler, tow-path walking. Finally, this is one of the few remaining districts in England and Wales where even the motorist can enjoy the high country in relative isolation. The minor road from Ystradfellte to Heol Senni across Fforest Fawr leads through a stretch of wild Wales. Even more spectacular is to walk from the 1464-foot summit along Sarn Helen south-west towards the Vale of Neath, 15 miles away.

The Brecon Beacons

Any walker or climber who is making a first visit to the Brecon Beacons should start by going to the Libanus Mountain Centre, south-west of Brecon. Not only is a wealth of information available here about the area, but the situation of the Centre itself, on a hill at 1100 feet, gives splendid views over the surrounding moorland. One of the many footpaths which is sure to be recommended is that to the summit of Pen y Fan, the highest peak in the National Park and in South Wales (2906 feet).

The Black Mountain, with Bannau Brycheiniog and Llyn y Fan Fawr.

The foot of the mountain lies 9 miles south-west of Brecon and the ascent track to the summit starts beside the Outdoor Pursuits Centre at Storey Arms. This is one of the most celebrated hill-tracks in Wales, giving some 3 miles of glorious walking. Although steep in places, the track is well marked and no scrambling is required. The reward from the flat-topped summit is superb vistas in every direction, especially to the north and west. Pen y Fan is itself a spectacular sight, its front cut by long gullies and covered in ribs of rock and grass.

The classic route in the Brecons is the traverse of the Cribin (2608 feet), Pen y Fan, and Corn Du (2863 feet) horseshoe. A degree of scrambling is involved and the full traverse is a strenuous day-long walk. There are yet more superb views at every point but it is not a route for the inexperienced nor one (like the ascent of Pen y Fan) to be tackled in bad weather. The popular ascent path begins at the access road to the Neuadd reservoirs, west of the three summits and north of Merthyr Tydfil.

The Black Mountains

East of the Brecon Beacons, on the other side of the Usk Valley, the Black Mountains rise in a series of whale-back ridges to the north of Abergavenny. The Gadair Ridge dominates the group, with Waun Fach the highest peak at 2660 feet. The range is superb walking country but care and skilful use of map and compass are necessary in poor weather as the summits are all roughly at the same altitude, making recognition of landmarks difficult.

There is quiet access to the Black Mountains from Hay-on-Wye. A minor road south of the town leads to a stretch of Offa's Dyke path, which proceeds to Hay Bluff (Pen y Beacon; 2219 feet), one of the most accessible summits in the range. This massive scarp provides stunning views deep into Central Wales and towards the Shropshire Hills in the north. From here the path continues south-east above the Honddu Valley along Hatterrall Ridge, the easternmost scarp of the Black Mountains, keeping above 2000 feet for some 4 miles.

The Crickhowell region is a strategic base from which to tackle the summits of the range, and the village itself is prettily located on the River Usk. Pen Cerig-calch looms just to the north, at 2302 feet. There is an alternative track from the hamlet of Cwmdu, 4 miles north-west, alongside the A479, to its even higher neighbour, Pen Allt-mawr (2360 feet). A scenic crest route traverses the range from Crickhowell, leading eventually to Grwyne Fawr reservoir, 11 miles to the north.

East of Crickhowell, to the north of the Usk Valley, the shapely mass of the Sugar Loaf mountain forms a familiar, and unmistakable, landmark. A variety of paths lead to the summit (1955 feet), all of them quite strenuous, but worthwhile for the rewarding view.

The Black Mountain

In the north-western corner of the National Park lies the Black Mountain, better (and less confusingly) known in Wales as 'Carmarthen Van'. This vast plateau of wild high moorland extends for 25 square miles between the A4067 and A4069 roads. The treeless moor of peat and bog is crowned by jagged sandstone ridges in the north-east. The highest point is on the steep crest of Bannau

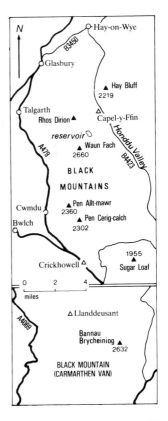

Brycheiniog (2632 feet) which affords extensive views. From the ridge, cliffs drop 500 feet into two isolated and beautiful tarns known in Welsh legend.

South of Llandovery, off the A4069, numerous hill-tracks lead up on to the western flanks of the Black Mountain. One landmark south-east of Llan-

Sugar Loaf from the south-west.

deilo is the ruined thirteenth-century Carreg-Cennen Castle, perched at 300 feet on top of a huge limestone crag. The Youth Hostel at Llanddeusant, south of Llandovery, is located strategically near several worthwhile walking objectives.

Climbing Information

1 The **old red sandstone** of the Brecon Beacons only offers reasonable climbing under winter conditions of snow and ice. Best are the N. face of Pen y Fan (012 216) and the gullies of Craig Cerrig-gleisiad (963 218).

2 The worthwhile rock climbing in the region is mainly in abandoned quarries in the **carboniferous limestone** belt lying along the southern fringe of the mountains. Most important:

● **Mynnydd Llangattock**: 3-m. escarpment at 1500 ft, fine situation 2 m. S. of Crickhowell. Most developed at G.R. 202 154 and more recently further E. Much scope elsewhere. Many climbs, 60 – 100 ft (all grades).

● **Taf Fechan Quarry** (062 104): 3 m. N. of Merthyr Tydfil. More than 40 climbs (all grades), up to 140 ft. Profusion of cracks, corners, and grooves in pleasant position above river valley.

● **Morlais Quarry, Faenor** (048 099): 2 m. N. of Merthyr. Some 65 climbs, all grades especially VD – S and up to 100 ft. N.-facing hillside above river.

● **Craig Taynau Gwynion** (065 105) close by; many short easier climbs.

● **Craig Cefn Coed** (035 081) some 2 m. NW. of Merthyr. Some 70 mainly easier climbs on 500 yds of cliff up to 120 ft high. Unfortunate setting partly beneath main highway flyover.

● **Dinas Rock** (913 080): 3 m. NW. of Hirwaun. Series of hard steep modern climbs up to 150 ft in pleasant setting.

● **Taff's Well Quarry** (128 828): 8 m. NW of Cardiff. Some 30 climbs (all grades) up to 150 ft.

The Cambrian Mountains

Essential Information

Height: Average between 1500 and 1900 ft; max. Pen Plynlimon Fawr (2468 ft)

Area: North–south 40 miles; east–west 15 miles

Distances from main towns: Aberystwyth 5 miles; Welshpool 9 miles; Carmarthen 20 miles

Suggested bases: Llanidloes, Aberystwyth, Rhayader

Access routes: A470/A489 (north) between Machynlleth and Newtown; A44/A470 (central) between Aberystwyth and Rhayader; A482 (south) between Llanwrda (south-west of Llandovery) and Lampeter

BR stations: Llandovery, Llandrindod Wells, Machynlleth, Caersws, Aberystwyth, Devil's Bridge

Youth hostels: Ystumtuen, Nant-y-Dernol, Blaencaron, Dolgoch, Tyncornel

OS maps: 135, 136, 146, 147

The Cambrian range, which occupies a dominant position in mid-Wales, is a wild region of bare hills, tortuous river valleys, and deep forests. It is the central region (east of a line between Lampeter and Machynlleth) that holds the most appeal for mountain-lovers. Within this wide band of upland territory there is wild beauty which is comparable, if not quite so spectacular, to that of neighbouring Snowdonia.

The southern Cambrians

If much of the Cambrians is comparatively little visited, the Devil's Bridge is a major Welsh tourist target. This should not deter the hill-walker from exploring the immediate surroundings which are themselves quite splendid; nor the beauty spot itself, where three bridges span the Mynach Falls. A toll must be paid to descend the ravine but it is worth it for the sight of the cascading River Mynach which, together with the Rheidol, has scoured chasms some 800 feet deep.

The footpath above Rheidol Gorge soon becomes free of crowds away from the main tourist centre. For distance-walkers there is a marked route via the Mynach and the upper Ystwyth Valley to Rhayader 20 miles to the south-east. This track passes through the Elan Valley among a series of reservoirs created for Birmingham Corporation. They are surprisingly well landscaped and harmonize well with the natural surroundings. There is walking of the gentler kind here, over 9 miles of water-side footpath, particularly accessible for those based at Rhayader.

South of Devil's Bridge, off the B4343 on the River Teifi, lie the ruins of the twelfth-century Cistercian abbey of Strata Florida, which in its day was compared to Westminster Abbey. Its location is close to the 4 square miles of Corsgoch Glan Teifi, the widest expanse of peat bog in Wales. This area is in general, however, one of rounded uplands, cross-hatched by wide wooded valleys. A track winds uphill to Llyn Teifi, 3 miles north-east of the abbey.

Plynlimon

Plynlimon, which rises to the north of the village of Ponterwyd, is in reality a series of smooth hills forming one vast upland plateau covered in peat bog. Numerous water-courses have their source on these slopes. The highest of the Plynlimon summits is Pen Plynlimon Fawr (2468 feet), which is also the highest point in the Cambrian Mountains. Two recognized routes lead to the summit: one from Eisteddfa Gurig farm alongside the A44,

83

5 miles north-east of Devil's Bridge, a fairly easy ascent; and the other from the Dyffryn Castell Hotel, which is longer and, unlike the other route, not marked. The wide panorama from the summit takes in mighty Cader Idris to the north

The Berwyn Mountains

The region around Llangollen, to the east of the Cambrian

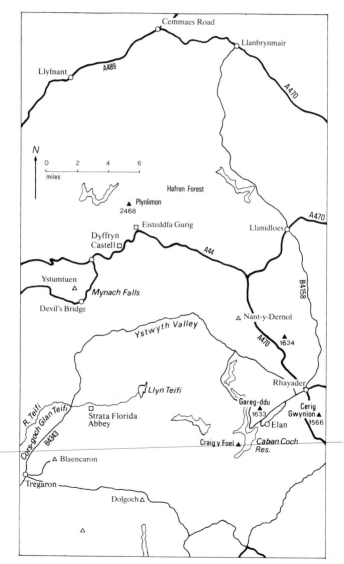

The Tregaron–Abergwesyn mountain road near Abergwesyn.

range, extending down to the Powys border, contains further hill ranges which remain unknown to the majority of walkers. The Berwyn Mountains, which curve to the south of the market town of Corwen, rising to 2712 feet, afford excellent ridge walking and good views which, in favourable conditions, extend as far as Snowdon. Scenic hill-paths lead to the remoter part of the range from the village of Cynwyd off the B4401 south of Corwen.

To the north-west of Llangollen on the northern side of the Dee Valley rises the Llantysilio Mountain; a path to the summit starts alongside the A542 in Horseshoe Pass.

Climbing Information

Not a rugged or rocky area and only occasional small crags provide limited climbing possibilities. The best, however, are worthwhile. In the Rhayader area some 8 m. W. of Llandrindod Wells, on **ordovician slate** are:

● **Garreg-ddu** (915 656): in Elan Valley 4 m. SW. of Rhayader village. Small crag in delightful situation overlooking Garreg-ddu Reservoir. A dozen climbs (all of easier grades) up to 200 ft.

● **Craig y Foel** (91 64): close by along the N. shore of Caban Coch Reservoir. Series of craglets provide easier climbs up to 100 ft.

● **Cerig Gwynion** (974 656) above confluence of Elan and Wye Rivers some 2 m. S. of Rhayader. Several climbs up to 100 ft on a steep and compact small crag.

● **Marteg** (952 714): series of craglets above confluence of Wye and Afon Marteg some 2 m. N. of Rhayader.

The Cumbrian Mountains

Essential Information

Height: Average between 1700 and 2500 ft; max. Scafell Pike (3210 ft)
Area: North–south 37 miles; east–west 30 miles
Distances from main towns: Penrith 5 miles; Carlisle 12 miles; Lancaster 22 miles
Suggested bases: Keswick, Wasdale Head, Patterdale, Skelwith Bridge
Access routes: A66 (north) between Penrith and Cockermouth; A595 and A5086 (west) between Millom and Cockermouth; A591 (central) between Windermere and Bothel; A592 (central) between Windermere and Penrith; M6 (east), exits 37–40; A6 (east) between Kendal and Penrith
BR stations: Kendal, Windermere, Penrith, Ravenglass
Youth hostels: Wastwater, Thirlmere, Patterdale (total of 31 within Lake District area)
OS maps: 89, 90, 96, 97

The impact of the Lake District on the first-time visitor is seldom less than astonishing as it seems scarcely credible that this mountainous region of jagged crags can be an integral

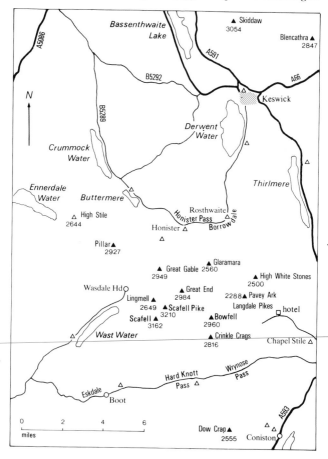

part of England's otherwise so gentle landscape. The igneous and metamorphic rocks – with volcanic debris and even limestones and sandstones – together with the radial group of lakes for which the region is named, are visually quite astounding.

Wasdale Head, Great Gable, Sty Head.

The oldest rocks – the Skiddaw Slates – are some 530 million years old and form the smooth, rounded northern mountains such as Skiddaw and Blencathra. The central area consists of the Borrowdale Volcanics, 500 million years old, and includes the Langdale and Scafell ranges. The gentler landscape to the south around Windermere is formed of Silurian Slate, the youngest of the rocks, some 420 million years old.

The Cumbrian Mountains enjoy real respect among climbers. The motorist sees relatively little of the dramatic heights, although some of the roads, such as those over the Kirkstone, Honister, Hard Knott, and Wrynose Passes, give a hint of the real majesty within close reach. Only at close quarters – on foot – is the truly awesome beauty revealed: below the Scafell summits or Langdale Pikes, on the top of Great Gable or Helvellyn, between Skiddaw and Blencathra.

This almost square-shaped National Park (England's largest at 866 square miles) is a virtual paradise for hill-walkers and climbers. The pedestrian explorer is also well served by a wealth of Information Centres, Outward Bound schools, defined tracks and climbing crags, Youth Hostels and camp grounds. Guided walks are becoming increasingly popular, indicating an awareness that the higher Lakeland regions are definitely not the

Scafell Pike above Hollow Stones cwm.

province of the novice.

The lakes themselves offer attractive and varied walking along the shoreline for the less experienced or less energetic. The circuit of Buttermere is one popular walk, and similarly around Grasmere and Wast Water. Windermere's western shoreline is also popular. The triangle encompassed by Windermere, Grasmere, and Coniston is only a small and crowded hub. The real high-country grandeur lies outside this tourist area, primarily to the north and north-west.

Some of the summits are quite readily accessible. The relatively easier ascents include Skiddaw (3054 feet), north of Keswick, and Helvellyn (3116 feet), reached from a 3-mile path off the A591 between Keswick and Grasmere. Patterdale, at the head of Ullswater and below the eastern flank of Helvellyn with its sensational Striding Edge route, is a popular base with hill-walkers. Eastwards is the remote High Street range (2719 feet), named for the Roman road that traces its crest, and westwards St Sunday Crag (2756 feet), overshadowed by the massive Helvellyn.

The Scafell range

There is no question about the

ultimate target of every walking enthusiast who visits the Lake District. It is the summit of Scafell Pike, England's highest mountain at 3210 feet, which rises above Wast Water in the south-western corner of the region. Scafell Pike is only one of a succession of peaks which form the Scafell range: Scafell (3162 feet), Great End (2984 feet), Lingmell (2649 feet) are some of the others, all worthy of exploration. In clear conditions the view from the summit of Scafell Pike is truly panoramic, and provides adequate reward for the effort of the ascent.

Pike o' Stickle (l), Harrison Stickle (r).

The most direct access route for the motorist is from the A595 coast road via Gosforth and Wasdale Head. For those approaching from the east from the central region of the Lake District, the route leads from Ambleside over Wrynose and Hard Knott Passes, through Eskdale to Wasdale Head. Wasdale has long been an important centre for climbing and walking, and is the most strategic base from which to make a wide variety of exhilarating and memorable expeditions into the surrounding mountain ranges.

The Gable group

To the north of Scafell Pike stands Great Gable (2949 feet), the most symmetrically perfect of England's peaks. This is another of the most popular of the Cumbrian summits, not least for the magnificent view which it affords, particularly towards the north-west where Skiddaw dominates the skyline. The ascent can be made by a variety of routes, of varying degrees of difficulty. For the less-experienced walker the least taxing route is from the top of Sty Head Pass, south of Borrowdale, following the marked path.

The mountain can also be approached from Wasdale Head, by a combination of routes. Another, longer, route starts from the top of Honister Pass; it passes through the quarry to the south of Honister Hause, skirts Grey Knotts (2287 feet), and leads on to Green Gable (2603 feet), then dropping into Windy Gap before ascending to the summit cairn on Great Gable.

The Langdale Pikes

The Langdale Pikes, to the west of Ambleside, share an almost equal popularity with the Scafell range. Access is via the B5343 from the A593 at Skelwith Bridge. There is ample accommodation throughout the whole Langdale area, and any of the points along the valley is well placed for ascents of the range. The principal peaks are Harrison Stickle (2401 feet), Pike o' Stickle (2323 feet), and Pavey Ark (2288 feet). To the north, above

Langdale. Stake Pass from Lining Crag.

the moorland known as High Raise, stand High White Stones (2500 feet).

The main starting-point is from the New Dungeon Ghyll Hotel, near the head of the dale, itself well known to many walkers and climbers who have found rest and refreshment there. Many routes lead up on to the tops, all revealing different and dramatic views: of Stickle Tarn in the heart of the group, of the craggy ridge of Pavey Ark above it (2288 feet), with the bold ledge of Jacks Rake.

The jagged faces of the Langdale Pikes are a great attraction for climbers, but the area is also much favoured by hill-walkers seeking the quieter, almost secret recesses of the Lake District.

Langdale is also an ideal base from which to tackle the Bowfell group of mountains which lie to the west. Bowfell dominates the range at 2960 feet, with Esk Pike (2903 feet) and the unmistakable stony ridge of Crinkle Crags (2816 feet) only two of the worthwhile objectives.

The outer summits

While the central region of the Lake District is the main draw, the outer areas are also extremely attractive and have much to offer walkers, particularly those in search of peace and solitude in summer. Shap Fell on the eastern fringes is one, and is rightly the province of hill-walkers, notably between Shap village and Haweswater via Swindale Beck. Diagonally distant, in the south-west, is the Furness Peninsula where the Cumbrian Mountains tumble to the sea. The heights of Black Combe and Bootle Fell comprise an impressive and little-visited corner of the Lake District.

Climbing Information

Contains much of the very best rock-climbing in Britain: it was here that the sport was born in 1886. Typically the crags are composed of the **rhyolites** etc. of the Borrowdale Volcanic Series, and tend to be smaller and less conspicuous than their Snowdonian counterparts. There are well over 1500 climbs described in guide-books; only the most important can be mentioned.

Wasdale area

● **Scafell Crag** (208 068): awesome cliff, greatest in Lakes, high up under summit of Scafell and 1¾ m. SE. of Wasdale Head. N.-facing. Many climbs (all standards) up to 450 ft.
*'Central Buttress': 470 ft. HVS (1914) – perhaps most famous climb in Lakes
*'Scafell Pinnacle via Slingsby's Chimney': 335 ft. D+ (1888)
● **The Napes** (211 099): series of ridges and walls high on S. face of Great Gable 1½ m. NW. of Wasdale Head. With nearby crag of **Kern Knotts**, holds over 70 climbs (all grades) up to 350 ft.
*'Tophet Wall': 265 ft. S. (1923)
*'Napes Needle + Needle Ridge': 325 ft. HVD + VD (1886 + 1884) – the climbs that started it all
● **Pillar Rock** (172 123): in forbidding situation on N. flank of Pillar Mountain high above remote Ennerdale, 2½ m. NW. of Wasdale Head. Complex free-standing buttress with several faces holds many climbs (all grades but the hardest), up to 500 ft in length.
*'Rib and Slab Climb': 300 ft. S. (1919)

Buttermere area

● **Eagle Crag** (172 145): stern N.-facing crag high up on High Stile Range 1½ m. S. of Buttermere village. Climbs tend to be harder grades.
*'Eagle Front': 495 ft. VS (1940)

Borrowdale area – a profusion of smallish crags at low altitude.

● **Shepherd's Crag** (264 185): delightfully situated crag some 300 ft high, rises from woods at only 700 ft altitude over S. end of Derwent-water 3 m. S. of Keswick. More than 35 climbs (all grades, especially easier ones).
*'Little Chamonix': 200 ft. VD. (1946)
● **Black Crag** (263 174): close by holds a dozen or so climbs (all grades).
*'Troutdale Pinnacle': 360 ft. VD+ (1914)
● **Raven Crag** (284 114): a broken-looking crag high up on N. flank of Glaramara 2½ m. S. of Rosthwaite village. 20 or more climbs (many easier grades).
*'Corvus': 450 ft. D. (1950)

Thirlmere area

● **Castle Rock of Triermain** (322 197): two separate buttresses at low altitude with easy access, 4 m. SE. of Keswick. Some 30 climbs, typically steep, exposed and hard, up to 300 ft.
*'Overhanging Bastion': 270 ft. VS (1939)

Langdale area – many cliffs, large and small, in popular valley.

● **Gimmer Crag** (273 030): imposing buttress with 3 faces and southerly aspect high up in Langdale Pikes, 2¾ m. W. of Chapel Stile village. Over 50 climbs (all grades), up to 250 ft but generally shorter.
*'Kipling Grove': 175 ft. HVS (1948)
● **Pavey Ark** (286 080): large cliff in fine position overlooking Stickle Tarn high in Langdale Pikes 2½ m. NW. of Chapel Stile. Vegetated appearance. Some 30 climbs (all grades), old and easy, or modern and very hard. Up to 300 ft.
*'Rake End Chimney': 165 ft. D. (1898)
● **Bowfell** (245 069): over 20 climbs (generally easier grades), up to 350 ft on high mountain crag just under summit of Bowfell and facing NE. some 5 m. W. of Chapel Stile.
*'Bowfell Buttress': 350 ft. D+ (1902)

Coniston area

● **Dow Crag** (263 978): mountain crag in fine setting 2½ m. W. of Coniston village. 4 main buttresses face E. and hold more than 50 climbs (all standards), up to 400 ft.
*'C. Ordinary Route': 360 ft. D. (1904)
*'Eliminate A': 375 ft. VS. (1923)

Snowdonia

Essential Information

Height: Average between 1950 and 2500 ft; max. Snowdon (Y Wyddfa; 3560 ft)

Area: North–south 45 miles; east–west 30 miles

Distances from main towns: Bangor 5 miles; Colwyn Bay 7 miles; Aberystwyth 15 miles

Suggested bases: Betws-y-coed, Beddgelert, Dolgellau

Access routes: A5 (north) between Betws-y-coed and Bangor; A498/ A4086 (central) between Porthmadog and Capel Curig; A470 (south) between Machynlleth and Ffestiniog

BR stations: Machynlleth, Bangor, Betws-y-coed, Porthmadog

Youth hostels: Pen-y-Pass, Oaklands (Betws-y-coed), Kings (Dolgellau) (total of 16 hostels in Snowdonia area)

OS maps: 115, 116, 124, 125, 135

Largely encompassed by Britain's second-largest National Park (838 square miles), the ranges of North Wales contain not only the highest mountain in England and Wales – Snowdon (Y Wyddfa) – but also thirteen other summits which rise to 3000 feet. Many are rather more challenging than Snowdon and more spectacular in shape and atmosphere.

There are eight distinct ranges within the region, five in the north and three in the south, the result of cataclysmic volcanic upheavals around 400 million years ago. The action of glaciers in the subsequent Ice Age and natural erosion have shaped the landscape as it is today: high mountain passes, rugged valleys, sharp ridges and rocky crags, still lakes and rushing cascades. This is true mountain country, its scenery varying only between the beautiful and the majestic, an acknowledged mecca for hill-

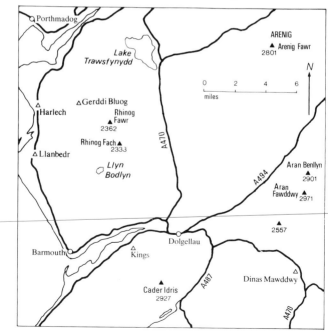

walkers and climbers.

Beddgelert, at the junction of the main A498 and A4085 roads, is an excellent base from which to explore a marvellous mixture of forest and mountain scenery. From here tracks lead to Snowdon, 5 miles to the north, while Moel Hebog (2568 feet) looms almost above the village. The ascent to this summit is both pleasant and easy, and the route can be extended to take in Moel yr Ogof (2020 feet) and Moel Lefn (2094 feet) to the north. The views from the summit of Moel Hebog are quite superb, over the Snowdon range and the Vale of Gwynant. For distance-walkers there is not only Beddgelert Forest which is crossed by many way-marked tracks, but Gwydyr Forest which spreads north-east in the Betws-y-coed area. This is an exhilarating un-broken tract of hill-country.

The Carneddau range

In the north of the region, the Carneddau range forms a massive landscape barrier between Betws-y-coed and the coast between Bangor and Conwy. For a preview, as it were, from the north, there is a 9-mile hill-track between Ty'n-y-groes and Aber on the A55. Once a Roman road, and rising to 1400 feet, this is a defined and fairly gentle introduction to the more regal heights (from 2000 feet of elevation). The Carneddau are splendid walking country; great whale-back grass-covered ridges with rock outcrops, they are the largest area of high ground in Snowdonia. The two highest peaks are Carnedd Llywelyn (3485 feet) and Carnedd Dafydd (3426 feet).

Penetrating deeper into the range demands stamina and expertise, especially to reach the summit of Carnedd Llywelyn. A favoured track is that which begins alongside Llyn Ogwen on the A5, but it is tough going, quite tricky in parts, and not the province of the beginner. This does not mean that the high places are inaccessible, for there are several beautiful valleys which indent the north-eastern flank of the range, ideal for walkers following water-courses like the Afon Dulyn from Tal-y-Bont on the B5106.

The Glyders

The main A5 road which threads its way north-west from Betws-y-coed to Bangor alongside the rivers Llugwy and Ogwen divides the Carnedau range from the Glyders. If the former are rugged, the latter are formid-able and include some of the most splintered and difficult climbing peaks in the British Isles. Even the easiest route to the isolated summit of Tryfan (3010 feet), with its three sharp peaks, demands rock-scram-bling, while the summit pla-teaux of Glyder Fach (3262 feet) and Glyder Fawr (3279

View south-east from Snowdon summit.

feet) – scattered with great blocks and flakes of rock – fall off northwards in a series of steep crags. In the heart of the group, moody Llyn Idwal is encircled by spectacular cliffs cleft by the famous Devil's Kitchen. An easy walk from Ogwen Cottage on the A5 leads to the lake.

Snowdon

Snowdon itself must be one of the most frequently climbed mountains in the world. A number of routes, all well defined, lead to the summit (3560 feet), which in good weather conditions affords an exhilarating panoramic view, as far as the Cumbrian Mountains and the Isle of Man. Two of the easy routes (excluding the path beside the rack-railway) are via the Pyg Track or the Miners' Track; they both begin at Pen-y-Pass, at 1170 feet on the summit of Llanberis Pass on the A4086 south-west of Capel Curig, and both routes are eminently suitable for beginners (in summer). Other pleasant routes are the 'Snowdon Ranger' from Llyn Cwellyn, the Watkin from Nant Gwynant, and the longer Beddgelert track.

For those who prefer more challenge and fewer crowds, the route over the sharp rocky ridge of Crib Goch is both physically exhilarating and visually spectacular. The traverse of the famous Horseshoe ridge in winter is sublimely beautiful, but it can be a serious undertaking and the hill-walker must be both suitably experienced and properly equipped.

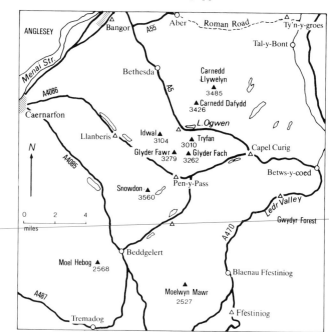

The Rhinogs

The rugged conformation of many of the Snowdonian mountains makes them popular with serious climbers, not least for their resemblance to greater ranges in other parts of the world. It is not for nothing that the Rhinogs, south of the Vale of Ffestiniog, have long been favoured by expedition teams in training. The range, still wild and remote, is especially rocky and jagged – although without major cliffs – and the going is consequently tough. The peaks of Rhinog Fawr (2362 feet) and Rhinog Fach (2333 feet) are separated by the high and desolate pass of Bwlch Drws Ardudwy, most easily reached by the minor road to Nantcol off the A496 at Llanbedr, south of Harlech.

Cader Idris

In the south of the National Park, below the beautiful Barmouth Estuary, lies Cader Idris (Arthur's Chair), second only to Snowdon as a magnet for walkers and climbers. The most popular ascent routes are via the Pony Track (2½ miles) or the Foxes' Path (2 miles), both of which start a couple of miles south-west of Dolgellau. There are at least six more alternative tracks to the summit ridge which stretches for some 8 miles. From the rocky summit at 2927 feet the distant views, particularly to the north, surpass even those from the top of Snowdon. There are many narrow ridges and precipitous cliffs which demand skill and experience, making Cader Idris yet another of the

Prospect eastwards up the Ogwen Valley from the top of Y Garn.

Welsh mountains worthy of respect, but rewarding in the most exhilarating manner.

The Arans

The Aran range of hills rises to the south of Snowdonia, to the north and east of Dolgellau. The highest peak, Aran Fawddwy, reaches 2971 feet, thus exceeding Cader Idris. Aran Fawddwy forms the southern point of the main summit ridge, and Aran Benllyn (2901 feet) the northern point. The ridge is easily accessible from the north, south, and west, but the eastern side (formed by Aran Benllyn) reveals a steep series of dark

Climbing Information

The region contains arguably the best rock-climbing in Britain, unsurpassed in quality and quantity. Most cliffs formed of **rhyolite, dolerite,** or associated lavas and tuffs of Snowdon Volcanic Series. Only the most important of many excellent crags in each mountain group can be included. There are over 100 cliffs in Snowdonia which have been described in guidebooks.

Carneddau

● **Craig yr Ysfa** (695 635): 1 m. SE. of Carnedd Llywelyn summit is huge vegetated rambling cliff facing E. over desolate Cwm Eigiau. Over 70 climbs (all standards), often on immense hidden gully walls.
*'Amphitheatre Buttress': 900 ft. VD (1905)
*'Mur y Niwl': 250 ft. VS (1952)

Glyders

● **Tryfan East Face** (664 594): falling from summit crest are 3 superb main buttresses and 3 lesser ones in unsurpassed situation – a true mountain wall. Face, some 700 ft high, holds over 50 climbs (mostly easier grades), rarely steep and of fine 'mountaineering' character.
*'Grooved Arete': 600 ft. VD (1911)
● **Idwal Slabs** (644 588): 1 m. S. of Ogwen Cottage on A5. Just one cliff in crag-girt hollow of Cwm Idwal, one of grandest cwms in Wales. A sheet of slabs and associated steep walls, of total height some 800 ft, provides more than 60 climbs of every shade of difficulty, many of them at easy standards.
*'Hope': 450 ft. VD (1915)
● **Clogwyn y Geifr** (639 589): the awesome cliff wall, split by the Devil's Kitchen, at the head of Cwm Idwal. Nearly 60 steep climbs (all grades), up to 300 ft high and plenty of atmosphere.
*'Devil's Staircase': 300 ft. S (1899) Mention should be made of finest scramble in area, often exposed and requiring steady head but no roped climbing, which traverses **Tryfan** by its N. and S. ridges, continuing to summit of **Glyder Fach** by its NE. or Bristly ridge.

Llanberis Pass

Divides Glyder Range from Snowdon massif. Narrow valley holds series of crags along both sides, those on N. jutting from large rugged hillside, those on S. often hidden in series of hanging cwms. Many, especially on N. side, very easy of access.
● **Dinas y Gromlech** (629 569): on N. side above Pont y Gromlech, 1½ m. W. of Pen y Pass, 4 m. SE. of Llanberis. Impressive angular cliff holds some 50 steep climbs (all grades), many very hard.
*'Flying Buttress': 300 ft. D (1931)
*'Cenotaph Corner': 120 ft. XS (1952) – perhaps most famous rock-climb in Britain
● **Dinas Mot** (626 563): eye-catching gable-end of Crib Goch N. ridge above Pont y Gromlech on S. side of valley. Over 30 climbs (mostly medium or hard grades). Total height of cliff some 600 ft.
*'Direct Route': 250 ft. VS (1930)

Snowdon Massif

● **Lliwedd** (623 534): S. arm of Snowdon Horseshoe, 1 m. SW. of Y Wyddfa. Massive N.-facing moun-

cliffs, more difficult of access. A pleasant route to the summit of Aran Fawddwy starts from Abercywarch, one mile north of Dinas Mawddwy on the A470. The views from the ridge are particularly rewarding to the west, encompassing Cader Idris and the Snowdonian peaks.

The summit ridge of Cader Idris.

tainside, ½ m. wide, 1000 ft high, holds over 80 climbs, generally of middle grades but all serious, finishing on summit crest. Strong mountaineering atmosphere.
*'Avalanche + Red Wall': 870 ft. HVD (1907)
● **Clogwyn Du'r Arddu** (600 550): high on N. flank of Snowdon's NW. ridge, 1 m. NW. of Y Wyddfa. Possibly the finest cliff in Wales, a magnificent precipice rearing above a tiny dark lake. 8 different buttresses or faces, each of completely different character and holding well over 100 climbs, all serious and exposed and none easy, many extremely difficult.
*'Great Slab': 600 ft. VS (1930)
*'White Slab': 570 ft. XS (1956)
*'Llithrig': 250 ft. HVS (1952)

South Snowdon

A large area containing both mountain crags and cliffs (usually smaller and steeper) at lower altitudes on the fringe of the higher ground.
● **Tremadoc** (545 411 – 577 406): a 2½ m. escarpment containing 4 ancient sea-cliffs rising steeply from woodland above A498 and A408 about 1 m. N. of Porthmadog. All face S. across flat farmland towards sea, extremely popular venue because of easy access and better weather than mountains. Approx. 150 climbs, mostly 100 – 200 ft, none easy, few middle grade, many VS and harder.
*'Creagh Ddu Wall': 200 ft. HS (1951) (Craig y Castell)
*'Vector': 250 ft. XS (1960) (Craig Bwlch y Moch)

Moelwyns

This range of E. Snowdonia holds several crags, the best some 1200 ft up on E. slopes above Tan y Grisiau. Typically they face SE., rise between 200 and 400 ft and hold climbs of all standards.

Rhinogs

Only two crags in the range, best known:
● **Craig Bodlyn** (650 237): 300-ft N.-facing cliff above remote Llyn Bodlyn some 4 m. SW. of Rhinog Fach. Holds some dozen climbs all in harder grades.

Cader Idris

Six main climbing crags on both N. and S. sides of mountain, all in superb settings. Best known are:
● **Cyfrwy** (703 135): 1 m. NW. of summit. Shapely and complex N.-facing crag over 600 ft high ending on a 2600-ft top; over 20 climbs (all grades).
*'Cyfrwy Arete': 450 ft. D (1888)
● **Craig Cau** (712 122): 1 m. S. of summit. Huge complex cliff nearly 1000 ft high but broken and vegetated. Faces NE. into wild cwm above Llyn Cau. Over 20 climbs (all standards).
*'Pencoed Pillar': 730 ft. HVD (1903)

Arans

Several crags, including:
● **Craig Cowarch** (848 193): 4 m. N. of Dinas Mawddwy an E.-facing hillside holds no fewer than 28 separate buttresses and faces spread over 1½ m. above attractive pastoral upland valley. Over 150 climbs (all grades) up to 500 ft in length.
*'Stygian Wall': 220 ft. VS (1955)

Queen Elizabeth Forest Park and the Trossachs

Essential Information

Height: Average between 1750 and 2200 ft; max. Ben Lomond (3192 ft)
Area: North-east to south-west 15 miles; north-west to south-east 15 miles
Distances from main towns: Glasgow 20 miles; Stirling 22 miles
Suggested bases: Callander, Rowardennan, Aberfoyle
Access routes: A821 (north) between Callander and the Trossachs; B837 (south-west) between Drymen and Rowardennan
BR stations: Balloch, Dunblane
Youth hostels: Rowardennan, Trossachs
OS maps: 56, 57

From the shores of Loch Lomond in the Queen Elizabeth Forest Park rises Ben Lomond (3192 feet), the highest peak in this central area of Scotland. The Park, a designated region of mountain and forest, is often the first objective north of the Clyde for lovers of wilder countryside.

The 45 000 acres of the Park provide walking through superb scenery amid pine forest along the eastern shores of Loch Lomond. A well-marked path runs through the centre of the Park, linking Rowardennan with the village of Aberfoyle, 13 miles to the east. The West Highland Way runs along the hillsides above the eastern shoreline; the stretch between Drymen and Rowardennan is notably attractive. From the Rowardennan Hotel there is one of the easiest, and shortest, ascents to the summit of Ben Lomond, via a 4-mile, well-marked track.

The scene hereabouts, on the eastern side of Loch Lomond, is one that contrasts quietly but impressively with the busy and often crowded west bank, which is traced by the A82 trunk road. For walkers who enjoy a challenge, there is a distinctly rougher stretch of the long-distance path north of Rowardennan. This high route along the Craig Rostan probes the secret hiding-place of the legendary hero Rob Roy.

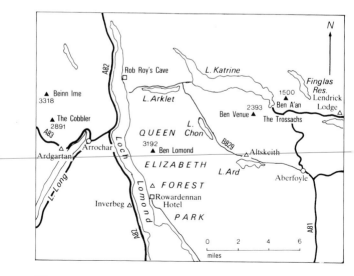

The Trossachs

Just to the north of Aberfoyle, beyond Achray Forest, lie the Trossachs. This cluster of needle-point peaks is situated within a great bowl of mightier mountains, foothills of the Grampians. The boundaries of the Trossachs are somewhat loosely defined as the area between Loch Lomond and Callander, but the heart lies around Loch Achray, with Ben A'an (1500 feet) rising on its northern side, and the rugged but beautiful Ben Venue (2393 feet) to the west.

This whole region is one of Scotland's famous beauty spots and as such caters well for walkers, climbers, and pony-trekkers. The lower slopes of the mountains are cloaked with birch and hazel trees, the tops rugged above the tree-line and often snow-capped till late spring. There are numerous established hill-tracks, especially from the shores of Loch Achray, which is itself flanked to the east by Loch Venachar and to the west by Loch Katrine. Loch Katrine offers the walker an interesting path which winds along the northern shore.

Aberfoyle is the acknowledged starting-point for several walks through the Trossachs, along way-marked routes established by the Forestry Commission. The Duke's Road and the David Marshall Forestry Lodge are two impressive attractions.

The Arrochar Alps

To the west of Loch Lomond lies further rich and varied scenery, notably the Arrochar Alps which rise above the northern end of Loch Long. The highest peak in the area is

Ben Lomond across Loch Lomond.

Beinn Ime (3318 feet), its summit affording magnificent views. Better known perhaps is the distinctive shape of The Cobbler (Ben Arthur; 2891 feet), situated 1½ miles south of Ben Ime above the shores of Loch Long. The classic ascent of The Cobbler is from the Forestry camp ground at Ardgartan. There is more fine walking along the old 'Rest and be Thankful' road, through the nearby Glen Croe, off the A83.

Climbing Information

Summer climbing; generally on small craglets of **mica-schist**:

● **Ben A'an** (505 083): mini-mountain only 1500 ft high 4½ m. N. of Aberfoyle; a dozen or so recorded climbs on S. face (generally easier grades) up to 100 ft in length.

● **Ben Ledi** (563 103): 4½ m. NW. of Callander; series of boulders and pinnacles to NE. of the 2873-ft summit give entertaining scrambles, problems, and short climbs.

● **Kilpatrick Hills: The Whangie** (494 796): a peculiar crevasse-like geological feature of smooth **porpherite** rock gives some 50 short and difficult climbs. A 'klettergarten' for Glasgow climbers.

● **Dumbarton Rock** (400 743): a headland on the Clyde shore in Dumbarton town, gives a couple of dozen climbs, all VS or harder and up to 100 ft or so but high quality on **basalt**. Also over 70 boulder problems, some quite long.

The Southern and Central Highlands

Essential Information

Height: Average between 2000 and 3300 ft; max. Ben Lawers (3984 ft)

Area: North–south 40 miles; east–west 30 miles

Distances from main towns: Stirling 14 miles; Perth 22 miles; Glasgow 28 miles

Suggested bases: Callander, Pitlochry, Aberfeldy

Access routes: A9 (east and north) between Dunkeld and Dalwhinnie; A827 (central) between Aberfeldy and Killin; A84/A85 between Callander and Crianlarich

BR stations: Dunblane, Tyndrum, Rannoch, Pitlochry, Dalwhinnie

Youth hostels: Killin, Crianlarich, Loch Ossian, Pitlochry

OS maps: 42, 43, 44, 50, 51, 52

The Grampians are not only the highest mountains in Britain, but they are by far the most extensive, straddling Scotland from the Firth of Forth to the Great Glen. Ben Nevis towers as almost the final summit, just east of the massive geological fault that divides the country between the Firth of Lorn on the Atlantic sea-board and the Moray Firth, an arm of the North Sea.

The central Grampians encompass a vast area between Callander and Glen Garry in the Forest of Atholl north-east of Loch Rannoch. From east to west the succession of ranges roll from Pitlochry to Loch Ericht and beyond. Roughly in the middle lies Ben Lawers, highest of the southern Highland peaks at 3984 feet, the giant of the Tayside region which dominates a magnificent 8000-acre National Nature Reserve.

Ben Lawers

The northern shores of Loch Tay have now become an established mountain playground under the protection of the National Trust for Scotland. On the slopes of the neighbouring Ben Ghlas there is a comprehensive visitor centre; from here a number of footpaths radiate across outstandingly lovely terrain, all offering sweeping vistas to the west and south. The grassy slopes of Ben Lawers provide a habitat for a wide and beautiful variety of plants including some rare alpine species.

The ascent path to the top of Ben Lawers starts from the car park some 5 miles east of Killin off the A827, the main road which runs below the southern flank of the mountain. The route is well defined and easy, and traverses Ben Ghlas (3740 feet) on its way to the summit ridge. On a clear day the views from Ben Lawers extend from the Atlantic to the North Sea.

Pitlochry area

North-east of Loch Tay stretches the richly wooded Tummel Valley around Pitlochry, an area of spectacular mountain heights and lovely

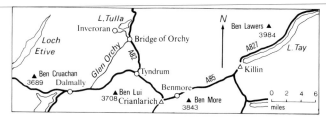

glens. Due north of Pitlochry lie the dramatic triple peaks of Beinn a'Ghlo (3671 feet). The group is accessible from the famous Pass of Killiecrankie which links Blair Atholl and Pitlochry. For the less-experienced walker, Ben Vrackie close to Pitlochry offers an inviting alternative, since the ascent path to the 2757-foot summit is both short and easy. The starting-point is at the hamlet of Moulin on the A924 just north of Pitlochry.

Forest of Atholl

North of Loch Rannoch lies some of the most majestic of all Scottish mountain scenery, encompassed by the Forest of Atholl which seems to stretch almost to infinity on either side of the A9 trunk road. The Garry Gorge is just one among a succession of wild and remote beauty spots. Here there are way-marked Forestry paths which quickly lead the walker away from the bustle of the main highway into tranquil seclusion. Dalwhinnie, at the head of Loch Ericht, is a popular base at all seasons of the year; in summer for its loch-side walks and tracks leading into the surrounding hills. Carn na Caim (3087 feet), A'Bhuidheanach Bheag (3064 feet), and Glas Mheall Mor (3037 feet), on the eastern side of the Pass of Drumochter, are some of the nearby heights.

The peaks of the Blackmount rising beyond Rannoch Moor.

Crianlarich area

Above: Ben Lui.
Below: View south-west towards Ben Cruachan.

In the Central Grampian area around Crianlarich, south-west of Loch Tay, rise two spectacular mountains. To the east of Crianlarich stands the prominent mass of Ben More (3843 feet), the main peak in a cluster of high mountains which mostly reach 3000 feet. In good conditions, the ascent of Ben More is easy and the views from the top are superb; the most popular starting-point

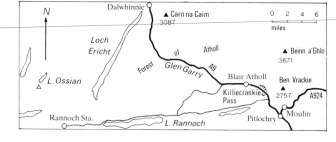

is from Benmore, 2 miles east of Crianlarich on the A85. The expedition can be extended to the summit of 'Stobinian' (3827 feet), but should only be undertaken by strong and experienced walkers.

The landscape west of Crianlarich is dominated by Ben Lui (3708 feet). The summit can be reached from the village of Tyndrum on the A82, or from further west on the A85 Oban road. The vista from the summit ridge is wide, reaching as far as Ben Nevis in the north.

Ben Cruachan

Further westwards, where the Grampians begin to tumble towards the great fjord of Loch Linnhe, the Pass of Brander cuts between Loch Awe and Loch Etive. Above it towers Ben Cruachan (3689 feet), a ridge with no less than seven peaks, with a reservoir and hydro-electric complex carved deep in its bowels. The summit of this striking mountain can be reached via the hydro service road and then by a 1½-mile track. The village of Dalmally, in a glorious setting among pine forest, is an excellent base, and also provides fine walking in Glen Orchy.

The West Highland Way

The long-distance path runs south to north through the Central and Strathclyde Regions from Inverarnan to Kingshouse near Glen Coe, covering some 32 miles via Glen Falloch and the old military road above Crianlarich. The route runs initially below forest, reaches over 1000 feet beyond Tyndrum, before traversing the great hillside of Ben Dorain (3524 feet). Now skirting Loch Tulla, the path enters the Highland Region among the peat uplands of Rannoch Moor, below the beautiful Blackmount peaks (3602 feet). This is hard walking among wild and desolate surroundings.

Climbing Information

Large tracts of this extensive area hold little or no serious climbing, although several mountains do hold a climb or two, usually **winter** routes, especially towards the W. beyond Rannoch Moor. There are 3 noteworthy **summer** areas:

● **Binnein Shuas** (468 826): some 12 m. E. of Roy Bridge. A fine crag of **micro-granite**, facing SE., holds more than a dozen good climbs up to 550 ft, at least one a classic.

● **The Cobbler** (259 059): some 2½ m. W. of Arrochar. The contorted crags of the Eastern corrie were the birthplace of hard Scottish rock-climbing between the Wars. Walls, buttresses, gullies, and chimneys give some 70 short **summer** climbs, on **mica-schist**, up to 350 ft (all grades). Also good short **winter** climbs when conditions are right.

● **Craig y Barns** (010 432): 1½ m. NW. of Dunkeld. A line of crags rising from woodland and facing S. and W. holds much popular climbing. **Metamorphic** rock provides interesting routes; easy access. Many of the Grampian Mountains provide excellent ski-mountaineering possibilities, especially:

Glas Maol (166 765): 1½ m. E. of Devil's Elbow on A93, gives superb 10-m. traverse N. to Lochnagar.

Beinn a'Ghlo (970 732): 10 m. N. of Pitlochry.

Ben Lawers (635 415): 6 m. NE. of Killin.

Grey Corries Group (Stob Coire Easain: 234 728): 5½ m. S. of Spean Bridge gives superb traverse.

Blackmount Group (Stob Ghabhar: 230 455): 6 m. NW. of Bridge of Orchy provides excellent traverse.

Ben More (433 245): 3 m. E. of Crianlarich, wonderful high-level traverse to **Stobinean**.

The Monadhliath Mountains

Essential Information

Height: Average between 2000 and 3000 ft; max. Creag Meagaidh (3700 ft)
Area: North-east to south-west 50 miles; north-west to south-east 20 miles
Distances from main towns: Inverness 8 miles; Fort William 10 miles
Suggested bases: Spean Bridge, Fort Augustus, Kingussie, Carrbridge
Access routes: A9 (north and east) between Dalwhinnie and Daviot; B862/B851 (west) between Fort Augustus and Daviot; A86 (south) between Spean Bridge and Newtonmore
BR stations: Dalwhinnie, Kingussie, Aviemore, Spean Bridge
Youth hostels: Kingussie, Aviemore, Inverness
OS maps: 34, 35

This huge upland area, still untouched by tourist development, is as yet virtually free of roads. The outer edges are accessible enough, but the heart of the Monadhliath Mountains remains almost empty. It is a rugged Highland fastness which is the domain of only the most adventurous climbers and hill-walkers.

The eastern group

Carrbridge, now an established ski-centre and mountain resort on the A9, provides good access to the north-eastern corner of the range. From here a minor road and track (and a historic one) winds alongside the River Dulnain west and then south-east between Carn Sleamhuinn (2217 feet) and Geal-charn Mor (2703 feet) to Aviemore, over a moorland and mountain route of 13 miles.

Between Carrbridge and Daviot, just off the A9, is Tomatin and Findhorn Bridge. South of here, the River Findhorn penetrates to the central Monadhliaths, traced for much of its length by service roads and tracks. Here are 10 miles or more of Scottish scenery at its wildest, between summits rising to 2500 feet and more.

The central group

A scenic (and relatively little-

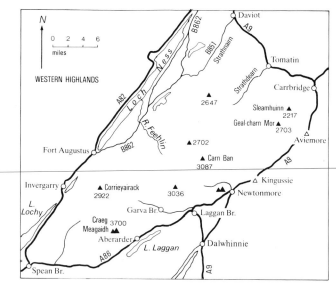

Creag Meagaidh seen up Coire Ardair.

used) minor road runs along the eastern side of Loch Ness, from Fort Augustus north to Daviot. This beautiful drive of some 30 miles along the western flank of the Monadhliaths provides a total contrast to the busy and sometimes very crowded A82 trunk road. From this minor road, tracks and service roads penetrate into the heart of the range, notably along the River Feehlin and in Strathnairn, near Daviot.

The western group

The most frequented route in the Monadhliaths is along General Wade's Road. The popular starting-point is west of Laggan Bridge, south-west of Aviemore. At Garva Bridge the road becomes a track and continues for 18 miles to Fort Augustus, crossing the rugged Corrieyairack Pass (2507 feet) on the way.

Newtonmore is beautifully located at the foot of Glen Banchor, and there is superb walking for those who explore the route of the River Calder. At the south-west corner lies Spean Bridge and, 3 miles east, off the A86 at Roybridge, Glen Roy with its curious 'Parallel Roads' – relics of Ice Age lake shores – high-level ledges on

hillsides either side of the valley.

Creag Meagaidh

The Monadhliath Mountains rise to their highest point on the summit of Creag Meagaidh (3700 feet), a complex mountain dominating the northern shores of Loch Laggan. An easy ascent path starts from Aberarder Farm off the A86, reaching in 4 miles a desolate corrie where a sweep of awesome 1500-foot cliffs – well known to climbers – tower above the waters of Lochan Coire Ardair. From the corrie the route runs via the 'Window' pass to the summit.

Climbing Information

● **Creag Meagaidh:** 14 m. W. of Spean Bridge. The huge NE.-facing **mica-schist** cliffs of Coire Ardair (435 875) are one of the finest **winter** climbing locations in Scotland. They extend nearly 2 m.; many climbs up to 1500 ft in height. Summer climbing unsatisfactory.

● **Creag Dhubh of Newtonmore** (668 958): a well-developed low-altitude, road-side crag of **mica-schist**, faces SE. in pleasant situation some 3 m. W. of Newtonmore on Speyside. Many steep **summer** rock-climbs up to about 300 ft.

The Cairngorms

The Cairngorms are a north-eastern sub-division of the Grampian chain, consisting of mountains which are only fractionally lower than the Nevis group to the south-west. Something the two ranges share at higher levels (altitude apart) is an 'arctic-alpine' climate: not surprising perhaps, since the latitude is roughly the same as that of Labrador in Canada to the west and the Russian Urals to the east. Untouched by the warming Gulf Stream that caresses the North-west Highlands, many high north-facing corries hold snow patches all year round. These are mountains which must always be treated as potentially hostile by the hill-walker or climber. Experience and skill with map and compass are vital to the safety and success of any expedition on to the Cairngorm plateau.

On the credit side, however, the Cairngorm region is one of

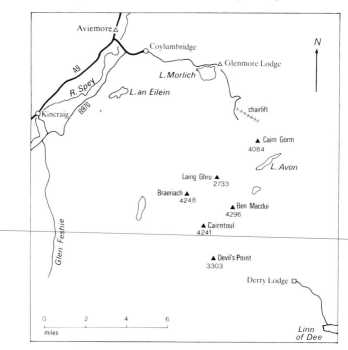

View over the Garbh Uisge.

regal splendour, in places quite breath-taking. No other mountain region in Britain offers so many outdoor leisure pursuits together with the organization to ensure safe enjoyment.

The Aviemore Centre, on the north-western side of the Cairngorm region, is an ideal base for those who like to balance spells in the wilder mountain areas with modern facilities. It is certainly the most popular base for winter visitors. Glenmore is another strategic centre, particularly for people who prefer simpler surroundings closer to the mountains in a setting of peaks, forest, and loch.

For the novice there is tuition in rock- and ice-climbing, downhill and nordic skiing and survival, canoeing, sailing, pony-trekking, and hill-walking, as well as nature studies and Outward Bound courses. For the individual wanderer, whatever the level of experience, there is a wide choice of way-marked forest trails and hill-paths, with easy access to high mountain levels via ski roads and lifts.

The Lairig Ghru

From Glenmore Information Centre in the heart of the Glen More Forest Park there are no less than eight magnificent way-marked trails, all relatively easy. In addition, and without doubt the most splendid, there is the trail through the famous defile of the Lairig Ghru – 'The Dark Pass'. The full traverse from Aviemore to Braemar, some 27 miles away, is as arduous as it is fascinating. The succession of high peaks enclosing the Lairig Ghru include Braeriach (4248 feet), Ben Macdui (4296 feet), and Cairntoul (4241 feet). This is a track much loved by backpackers, involving a stern and challenging walk, but no climbing. The descent from the high pass to Braemar below The Devil's Point (3303 feet) is particularly memorable.

Wildlife enthusiasts also have good reason to explore this mountain range, for the forest park contains the largest nature reserve in Britain, containing rare animals and birds like the Highland Wild Cat, the Golden Eagle, and the Osprey. In summer the higher corries are bright with alpine flowers; the nature trail established at

Coire an t-Sneachda.

Loch an Eilein (3 miles south of Aviemore) reveals the identity of most species of flora and fauna to be found among the quieter high places.

Ben Macdui

The Cairngorms rise to their highest point on the remote summit of Ben Macdui (4296 feet), the second-highest peak in Britain. Ben Macdui is part of a vast massif which dominates the Central Cairngorms and includes Cairn Gorm (4084 feet) on the northern edge; a high plateau joins the two peaks. The ascent of Ben Macdui is not difficult, but any

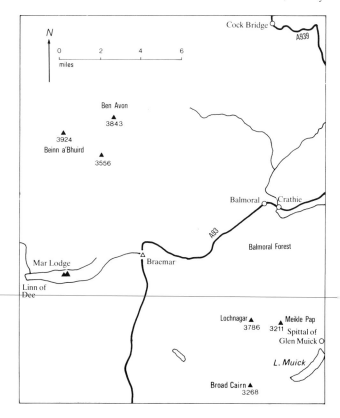

of the routes to the summit is of necessity long.

Braemar area

Lochnagar, north-eastern Scotland's most famous mountain which dominates the landscape in the Royal Estate of Balmoral, is an almost obligatory target for lovers of high places. From Braemar a road runs via Balmoral through Ballater to the Spittal of Glen Muick. A defined track ascends for some 5 miles from this beautiful glen over the shoulder of Meikle Pap (3211 feet) and along the edge of the impressive red granite cliffs which enclose the tiny lochan to the 3786-foot summit. While the ascent is not difficult, care should be taken near the cliff edge, especially in mist or when snow is still lying.

Equally dramatic, but gentler is the Linn of Dee to the west of Braemar village. From Mar Lodge Winter Sports Centre, footpaths probe into the mountains along the pine-edged river. The combination of cascading white water, forest, and mountain backdrop add up to a scene of great beauty. Some 20 miles north-east of here, on the A939, lies Tomintoul, at 1124 feet the highest village in the Highlands. This is a strategic base from which to explore the wooded Strath Avon and nearby Glenlivet.

Climbing Information

Best known for their winter climbing, which is more dependable than in most other regions because of geographical location and altitude. Also many excellent summer rock-climbs on steep black **granite** on the many cliffs throughout the range.

● **Creag an Dubh Loch** (235 824): largest cliff in Cairngorms, remotely situated 12 m. SE. of Ballater on N. Ridge of Broad Cairn. Climbs up to 1200 ft in length on cliff extending 3/4 m. Fine **summer** and **winter** climbing (NE. facing).

● **Lochnagar – NE. Corrie** (250 855): high N.-facing crag some 6 m. S. of Balmoral. 3/4 m. of steep cliffs hold climbs up to 1000 ft long. Possibly best **winter** climbing in region also many classic **summer** climbs.

● **Loch Avon Horseshoe** (000 106): a series of fine crags surround this remote corrie at W. end of the Loch Avon some 10 m. SE. of Aviemore, especially:
Cairn Etchachan (004 015): fine **summer** and **winter** climbs up to 950 ft (N. facing).
Shelter Stone Crag (002 015): awesome pillar-like buttress holding superb and difficult **summer** and **winter** climbs up to 900 ft in length (NE. facing).
Hells Lum Crag (996 017): fine **summer** rock-climbs and **winter** ice routes up to 600 ft (SE. facing).

● **Northern Corries of Cairngorm:** two fine N.-facing crags both with easy access hold both good **winter** and **summer** climbs (many easier grades). Very popular. Some 8 m. SE. of Aviemore. Crags are: **Coire an t-Sneachda** (994 032) and **Coire an Lochain** (985 029).

● **Cairntoul/Braeriach Amphitheatre** (surrounding 955 985): very remote situation some 10 m. S. of Aviemore. At extremely high altitude, this is where the last glaciers in Britain finally melted apparently! A series of adjoining corries, including the famous **Garbh Coire Mor** (955 999) and **Coire Bhrochain** (942 979) hold many fine **summer** and **winter** climbs, the latter being especially good, up to 1500 ft but mostly around 500–600 ft.

Being basically high plateau country, the Cairngorms offer excellent ski mountaineering; the traverse of the four 4000-ft tops is an especially noteworthy expedition.

Glen Nevis and Glen Coe

Essential Information

Height: Average between 2500 and 3600 ft; max. Ben Nevis (4406 ft)
Area: North–south 20 miles; east–west 16 miles
Distances from main towns: Fort William 2 miles; Oban 25 miles; Inverness 66 miles
Suggested bases: Fort William, Glencoe
Access routes: A82 (south and west) between Glen Coe and Fort William; A86 (north) between Tulloch and Spean Bridge
BR stations: Fort William, Tulloch, Corrour
Youth hostels: Glen Nevis, Loch Ossian, Glen Coe
OS map: 41

This western region of the Central Highlands may not be extensive in terms of area, but it does contain no less than three of the seven British peaks which top 4000 feet, as well as some of the most awesome. Loch Leven runs from west to east, dividing the Glen Coe mountain groups in the south from the more open Mamores and the Nevis range which rise to the north.

Glen Coe

The open, heather-clad expanse of Rannoch Moor separates Glen Coe from the central ranges and provides an effective visual contrast which gives the peaks which flank the Glen even greater dramatic pro-

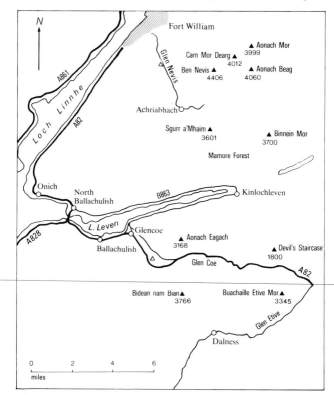

The North face of Ben Nevis.

minence. Volcanic in origin and massive in conformation, the sinister, even claustrophic, canyon can be as oppressive in gloomy weather as it is stimulating in bright light. Exciting peaks and interesting corries line the Glen, offering challenges to both climbers and hill-walkers. This is a stretch of truly wild Scotland, a world of gigantic boulders, white-water torrents, and great gullies clearing sheer rock walls.

On its southern side, Glen Coe is bounded by a string of regal peaks. The Bidean nam Bian massif (3766 feet), with its three spurs known as The Three Sisters, dominates the landscape at the western end. Several straightforward ascent routes start near the Clachaig Inn. At the eastern end of Glen Coe stands Buachaille Etive Mor (3345 feet) – 'The Great Shepherd' – a fitting guardian of the lovely Glen Etive, which opens to the south. A steep and craggy peak, the easiest ascent involves some scrambling.

The great 5-mile ridge of Aonach Eagach, which rises to 3168 feet at its highest point, forms the northern wall of the Glen. Its gullies and pinnacles are well known to climbers. The traverse of the ridge, best taken from the west, is narrow and exposed, and not for the inexperienced.

Glen Coe has an excellent Visitor Centre alongside the A82 which provides comprehensive information on hill-paths and climbing routes, as well as facilities for lightweight campers. First-time visitors should enquire here before exploring these mountains which are serious and should not be underestimated. Glencoe village has become a popular gathering place for high-country wanderers and climbers.

The Mamores

North of Glen Coe, on the northern side of Loch Leven, lie the Mamores, extending east–west for some 10 miles. The range reaches its highest point on the summit of Binnein Mor (3700 feet), which offers a wide panorama, with a particularly fine view of Ben Nevis to the north. The main ridge of

111

The view westwards down Glen Coe.

the Mamores offers some 7 miles of splendid high-level walking. There is access to the range from the north in Glen Nevis or from the south from the Old Military Road. A popular path to the summit of Sgurr a'Mhaim (3601 feet) begins from the farm-track at Achriabhach, 2½ miles south-east of Glen Nevis Youth Hostel.

Glen Nevis

To the north, the Mamores are bounded by Glen Nevis; prettier, and infinitely more friendly, than Glen Coe, at least at the western end close to Fort William. The vast slopes rising unbroken over 4000 feet from the floor of the Glen to the summit of Ben Nevis are the highest in Britain. Numerous hill-tracks lead into the recesses of the Glen and on into the surrounding area, notably along the Water of Nevis and south into the Mamores. Beyond the road head a gorge and fine waterfalls lead into the tranquil upper Glen.

The summit of Ben Nevis is

usually approached from Achintee up a minor road near the entrance to the Glen, or from the Glen Nevis Youth Hostel. While the ascent is easy, it is long and gruelling, yet many thousands reach the top of this, the highest mountain in Britain, each summer.

The ascent, via the Achintee path, over the shoulder of Meall an t'Suidhe (2322 feet) and up the rough zigzag trail to the summit cairn at 4406 feet, may take some 4 hours. Although the mountain is snow-bound into the early summer, and frequently hidden in cloud, on a clear day the views from the summit extend from the Cairngorms as far as the Western Isles.

Nevertheless, the Ben Nevis is a formidable mountain, and its awesome north-east face, over 2 miles of cliffs up to 2000 feet in height, holds climbs – especially ice routes – of world repute. The cliffs fall sheer from the plateau edge close by the summit, and those ascending by the easy trail should steer well clear. (Remember, too, that at 4000 feet the weather can be sudden and ferocious and snow may fall even in August.)

Eastwards, the wild and un-frequented peaks of Carn Mor Dearg (4012 feet) – which give a fantastic view of the cliffs of Ben Nevis – and Aonach Beag (4060 feet), Aonach Mor (3999 feet), and the 'Grey Corries' give wonderful ridge walking.

The West Highland Way

From the head of Glen Coe, the West Highland Way zigzags to the top of the Devil's Staircase at 1800 feet – the highest point of the long-distance path – before dropping to Kinloch-leven and skirting the Mamores along the Old Military Road to finish below Ben Nevis, 95 miles from its starting-point.

Climbing Information
Ben Nevis

4¼ m. SE. of Fort William. Private S.M.C. climbing hut below cliffs is at G.R. 166 723. Altitude and prox-imity to the Atlantic expose the Ben to weather conditions – both in winter and summer – that are unique in Europe. The scale of the mountain is truly alpine. Its huge NE. face (extending some 2 m. and up to 2000 ft high) is Britain's greatest cliff. It is a complex of ridges, buttresses, walls, and gullies: the rock is smooth volcanic **porphyry**. There are well over 200 climbs on the NE. face, many famous and classic and of world class. Excellent **summer** climbing. Superlative **winter** climbing. All routes (even the easy ones) are serious undertakings. There are a further 50 or so **summer** rock-climbs on Polldubh Crags (150 686): shorter, low-altitude crags on S. flanks of Ben Nevis in Glen Nevis some 4½ m. SE. of Fort William.

Glencoe

● **Buachaille Etive Mor** (223 545): this shapely peak, some 8 m. E. of Glencoe village, holds nearly 200 separate climbs on its complex N., E., and S. faces. Rock is a reliable **rhyolite**. Climbs (all grades) from 150 ft to 1400 ft in length, but most classics are around 500–700 ft; cliffs easily accessible from the road and offer first-class routes in both **summer** and **winter**.
● **Etive Slabs** (Beinn Trilleachan) remotely situated at G.R. 091 429,

yet easily accessible only 2 m. S. of the head of Loch Etive. Some 6 acres of pink **granite** slabs set at angle of some 40° only about 700 ft above the sea. Series of excellent friction climbs up to 1400 ft in length, usually 600–700 (mostly harder grades). SE. facing, beautiful situation; **summer** climbing only.
● **Bidean nam Bian** massif: 4 m. SE. of Glencoe village at 144 543 holds many different crags and gullies among its 3 northern corries, on its 3 northern ridges, and on its sub-sidiary summits. Rock is volcanic and generally **rhyolite** and **andesite**. Although all cliffs give **summer** and **winter** climbing, that for which the cliff is best known is given. Main areas:
Bidean (143 544): two very high buttresses just under summit on N. side hold dozen climbs 300–700 ft; classics in **summer** and **winter** conditions.
Stob Coire nam Beith (139 548): some 15 climbs on N. face 600–1500 ft, primarily **winter** climbs.
Stob Coire nan Lochan (148 549): more than 20 climbs of 400–500 ft on N. cliffs; high altitude; primarily **winter** climbs.
Aonach Dubh (150 559): over 100 climbs, primarily **summer** routes of 150–700 ft (all grades) on W., N., and E. faces.
Gearr Aonach (160 555): some 30 climbs on E. and N. faces, primarily **summer** routes of 300–400 ft.
Lost Valley (Coire Gabhail) (155 544): over a dozen **winter** climbs, generally 300–400 ft.

Glen Cannich, Glen Affric, Glen Shiel

Essential Information

Height: Average between 2000 and 3500 ft; max Carn Eige (3877 ft)
Area: North–south 25 miles; east–west 25 miles
Distances from main towns: Fort William 23 miles; Inverness 22 miles
Suggested bases: Dornie, Shiel Bridge, Cannich, Drumnadrochit
Access routes: A87 (south and west) between Invergarry and Dornie; A831 (north-east) between Drumnadrochit and Cannich
BR stations: Inverness, Muir of Ord
Youth hostels: Cannich, Glen Affric, Loch Ness
OS maps: 25, 26, 33, 34

North of the Great Glen, sandwiched between Loch Ness and the splintered west coast, lie 400 square miles of outstanding high country spanned east to west by a single road, the A87. This glorious hinterland of mountains and glens remains relatively free of holiday crowds. Those in search of true wilderness will find it within the deeper recesses of Glen Cannich and Glen Affric. Access is via Glen Urquhart and Cannich on the A831; from here two minor roads run alongside the rivers Cannich and Affric, then continue as tracks into country still largely untamed.

Glen Cannich

Loch Mullardoch (where the minor road from Cannich ends) is surrounded by towering peaks hung with fine deep corries. Over the northern shore of the loch towers Sgurr na Lapaich (3773 feet), while the southern shore is dominated by Carn Eige (3877 feet). For the distance-walker there is a winding and arduous route

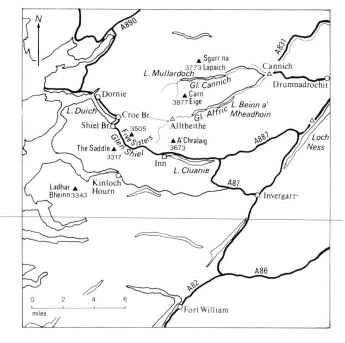

114

westwards which links eventually with a track and minor road to Dornie, some 17 miles away. A diversion southwards from the western end of little Loch na Lettreach leads to the impressive Falls of Glomach, at over 350 feet claimed to be the highest in Britain.

Glen Affric

Glen Affric, to the south-west of Cannich village, contains two lochs – Loch Beinn a'Mheadhoin (or, Benevean) and Loch Affric – as well as beautiful scenery of wooded glades and sparkling cascades. The recognized walker's route runs from Glen Affric to Croe Bridge, 18 miles away on the shores of Loch Duich. There is access for cars to the western end of Loch Benevean; from here, defined forestry roads and tracks lead to the secluded Youth Hostel of Alltbeithe and beyond through Kintail Forest below the northern slopes of the Five Sisters of Kintail.

This line of shapely peaks stretches from the head of Loch Duich along the northern side of Glen Shiel, rising to their highest point at Sgurr Fhuaran (3505 feet). Access is best from the A87 on the western flank of the range, where a track starts 1½ miles south of Shiel Bridge. The traverse of all Five Sisters is both long and ambitious, though the views from the ridge are well worth the effort.

Glen Shiel

Glen Shiel boasts further peaks, all equally impressive. On the southern side of the Glen, both The Saddle (3317 feet) and the Maol Chinn-dearg ridge (3200 feet) – over 5 miles long – hold superb high-level walking. At its eastern end, the Glen cul-

Glen Affric.

minates in Loch Cluanie, whose northern shore offers access to further high peaks. A'Chralaig (3673 feet) can be scaled from an ascent path which begins close to the Cluanie Inn at the eastern end of the Loch. Another route, to the summit of the neighbouring Sgurr nan Conbhairean (3635 feet), leaves the road 3 miles further east.

Climbing Information

Very rugged country with many crags and craglets but few satisfactory summer rock-climbs have been discovered (one exception below). Some good **winter** climbs: e.g. 1200-ft **mica-schist** cliffs of NE. face of **Ladhar Bheinn** (3343 ft) (827 038), an extremely remote peak some 8 m. W. of Kinloch Hourn. Good winter conditions very rare on this western seaboard.

● **Garbh Bheinn of Ardgour** (904 622): some 7 m. SW. of Corran Ferry. The huge remote NE. and E. faces of this 2903-ft mountain hold splendid cliffs of coarse **gneiss** and **quartzite**. More than 30 excellent **summer** rock-climbs have been made up to 1200 ft in length (all standards): the classics are among the best of their kind in Scotland.

The Torridons and Wester Ross

Essential Information

Height: Average between 2200 and 3200 ft; max. Bidein a'Ghlas Thuill (3483 ft)
Area: North–south 30 miles; east–west 25 miles
Distances from main towns: Ullapool 7 miles; Dingwall 25 miles
Suggested bases: Kinlochewe, Shieldaig, Achnasheen
Access routes: A832 (central) between Garve and Gairloch; A890 (south) between Strathcannon and Achnasheen; A835 (north) between Garve and Ullapool
BR stations: Strathcarron, Achnasheen, Garve
Youth hostels: Torridon, Craig, Ullapool, Aultbea, Gairloch
OS maps: 19, 20, 24

Some of the oldest sandstone rocks in Britain contribute to the grand geological conformation of the Torridons. Often capped with glittering white quartzite deposits, they glow uniquely in certain lights. This all adds to the natural scenic drama of the area which is very thinly populated. In this wide and wild spread of mountains and lochs, the landscape has in the main been spared any noticeable exploitation, making it a perfect location for a nature reserve covering some 10 000 acres. Walks and trails to match all levels of expertise and enthusiasm have been established by the National Trust for Scotland and the Forestry Commission.

Upper Loch Torridon

The most popular, and most visited, area of the Torridon massif lies to the west of Achnasheen, sandwiched between the hugh lochs of Torridon and Maree. Beinn

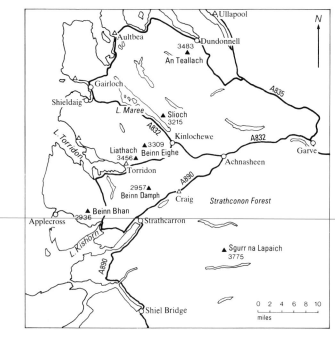

The summit crest of Liathach.

Eighe, to the west of Kinlochewe, is the largest of the Torridon peaks. It is a vast and impressive massif, its long narrow crest holding no less than nine separate summits, its slopes covered with quartzite screes. The eastern flank of the range has been designated a National Nature Reserve, where walkers may be fortunate enough to catch a glimpse of the protected Highland Wild Cat or the Pine Marten. The full traverse of the massif is a strenuous expedition of some 10 miles road to road which should only be tackled by strong and experienced walkers. Cromasag is the usual starting-point. Ruadh-Stac Mor (3309 feet), the highest top, stands on a spur north of the main ridge. Beinn Eighe is popular with both walkers and climbers; once the higher elevations are achieved it is not difficult to traverse from one top to another.

Further west along Glen Torridon, the landscape is dominated by the precipitous red sandstone cliffs of Liathach, capped with quartzite, which flank the northern side of the Glen. The narrow summit ridge, which rises to 3456 feet, is pinnacled and rather more difficult than Beinn Eighe, but provides exhilarating views throughout the whole of its length. Like Beinn Eighe, the full traverse over all seven summits, a distance of 6 miles road to road, calls for stamina and skill.

North-west of Liathach, separated from it by a deep glen, rises Beinn Alligin, the westernmost peak of the Torridons. The highest of the four tops is Sgurr Mhor (3232 feet). The usual starting-point of the ascent of Beinn Alligin is 2 miles west of Torridon village. The most difficult part of the ridge route is in negotiating the triple Horns of Alligin, situated at the far north-eastern end of the 2½-mile ridge, where care is required.

On the southern side of Upper Loch Torridon is the tiny fishing hamlet of Shieldaig. This is an excellent base in a quiet and beautiful location from which to make a variety of walking expeditions, particularly eastwards around Loch Damh. Ben-Damph Forest is

117

crisscrossed by numerous stalkers' tracks which provide good access to its various peaks, including the high ridge of Beinn Damph (2957 feet). There are also some fine and remote peaks in the adjoining Coulin Forest.

Applecross

Between Loch Torridon and Loch Kishorn, and also easily accessible from Shieldaig, is the beautiful Applecross peninsula. The spectacular and narrow road to Applecross village over the Bealach na Ba (2053 feet) is the highest in Britain, and from its summit a short ascent leads to Sgurr a' Chaorachain (2600 feet). This fine mountain and its neigh-

Slioch, rising sheer above the eastern shores of Loch Maree.

bour Beinn Bhan (2936 feet) provide magnificent panoramas over the sea to Skye and the Outer Hebrides while holding, on their eastern flanks, a series of awesome crag-girt corries – among the most impressive in Britain. A long but easy traverse links their wide summit crests.

Slioch

The regal waters of Loch Maree, studded with islets in its northern half, stretch for some 12 miles north-west of Kinlochewe, the western shore traced for almost all its length by the A832. To the south of the loch, the Nature Conservancy authority has provided nature trails and a visitor centre. The eastern shoreline is dominated by the square-topped bulk of Slioch, which

rises sheer to 3217 feet. The straightforward ascent starts from Glen Bianasdail round the head of the loch. The wild country to the north-east contains more than a dozen fine peaks and is known as 'The Great Wilderness'. Bordering the area on the north is An Teallach.

An Teallach

Due south of Little Loch Broom stands the jagged sandstone crest of An Teallach, a spectacular ridge with ten summits, which tops 3483 feet at its highest point, Bidean a' Ghlas Thuill. A 5-mile hill-track to the main summit starts near the Dundonnell Hotel. The traverse of the entire ridge involves some exposed scrambling. Although it can be avoided if really necessary, it should not be undertaken by the inexperienced. The splendid panoramas from the ridge extend north to the Summer Isles.

Climbing Information

While many mountains in this area offer some good climbs, in gullies, and on buttresses or ridges (especially under **winter** conditions), there are comparatively few major 'concentrations' of climbing; exceptions below. But much scope for exploration and real mountaineering combining walking, scrambling, and climbing.

● **Applecross:** climbs here on **Torridonian sandstone**. The **winter** climbing can be fantastic but good snow/ice conditions are rare.
Sgurr a' Chaorachain – 'The Cioch' (794 426): some 7 m. SW. of Shieldaig. Over a dozen **summer** climbs up to 1000 ft but mostly around 500 ft (all grades) on this extremely impressive feature on E. face of mountain. Some are among best sandstone climbs in Britain. S. face (792 414) holds six buttresses with easy access from road just below. A dozen good climbs in **summer** up to 650 ft.

Beinn Bhan: summer climbing is concentrated, so far, in Coire na Poite (808 450) 5½ m. S. of Shieldaig with several 500-ft climbs. But superb **winter** climbs have been made, up to 1400 ft, in the five E. corries.

● **Coulin Forest:** several cliffs of **Torridonian sandstone** where many climbs have been made, mostly in **summer** conditions but good **winter** potential. One cliff is famous:

Fuar Tholl (2968 ft) – Mainreachan Buttress (968 501): 2 m. NW. of Achnashellach station. Superb **summer** climbs, up to 700 ft and not easy, among the best in Britain of their kind.

● **Torridon:** much scope for **summer** and **winter** climbs, especially in Coire na Caime (922 578) on N. flank of Liathach. The famous cliff is:

Beinn Eighe – Coire Mhic Fhearchair (945 602): some 5½ m. W. of Kinlochewe. This awesome corrie holds three huge tombstone-like buttresses, facing N. Lower half of each is red **Torridonian sandstone**, top half white **quartzite**. More than 30 **summer** climbs, up to 1000 ft (all standards). Good **winter** climbs here also.

● **Letterewe:** this remote area, some 10 m. N. of Kinlochewe, is one of the most spectacular rock-climbing areas in Britain. Access is not easy. Noted for its **summer** climbs, but **winter** potential is great. Four huge cliffs and many lesser ones cluster near the Carnmore shooting lodge and the S. end of Fionn Loch. Main crags on NE. slopes of **Beinn Lair** (982 733) and SW. slopes of **A'Mhaighdean** (008 749) and **Beinn a' Chaisgein Mor** (Carnmore Crag – 980 773 – and Torr na h'Iolaire – 984 773). Over 150 recorded climbs, many now famous (all grades), up to 1400 ft in length, on **hornblende schist, gneiss,** or **sandstone**.

The Northern Highlands

Essential Information

Height: Average between 2400 ft and 3100 ft; max. Ben More Assynt (3273 ft)
Area: North–south 40 miles; east–west 30 miles
Distances from main towns: Inverness 60 miles (Ullapool), 100 miles (Lochinver)
Suggested bases: Ullapool, Lochinver
Access routes: A832/A835 (south and east) between Inverness and Ullapool; A836/A837 between Dingwall and Lochinver; A836/A838 between Dingwall and Durness
BR stations: Garve, Bonar Bridge, Lairg
Youth hostels: Ullapool, Achininver, Durness, Tongue
OS maps: 9, 10, 15

Coigach and Assynt

This empty wilderness at the far north-western corner of Britain is one of the most hauntingly beautiful areas of the kingdom. There are few roads and fewer signs of human life.

The land is wild moors – mapped as a jumble of tiny contour rings – and appears almost treeless, though green birchwoods nestle in sheltered hollows. The coast is deeply indented and garlanded with small islands. The climate seems more benevolent than further south and the skies wider.

The stately massif of Ben More Coigach (2438 feet) guards the route north from Ullapool. An interesting footpath crosses its great southern ramparts linking Culnacraig to the A835 at Strath Kanaird (above the island-studded sea).

Northwards rear six of the most spectacular peaks in Britain, each isolated and alone, crests of Torridonian sandstone – some even capped with white quartzite. From their narrow summits the wide moorland beneath seems more loch and river than terra firma. Stac Pollaidh (2009 feet) is a wonderful little mountain of weird pinnacles and crags, but its easiest ascent, by one of the scree gullies on the south face, is for scramblers only.

Rugged Cul Mor (2786 feet)

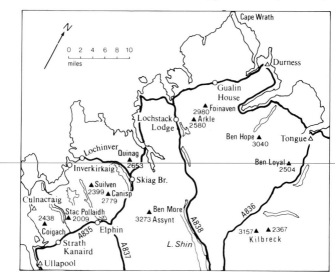

Stac Pollaidh from the west.

and Cul Beag (2523 feet) hold steep cliffs on the west but both tops can be reached from the A835 by their straightforward eastern flanks. The views are superb.

Known as 'The Matterhorn of Sutherland' when seen end-on from west or east, Suilven (2399 feet) is another remarkable peak. The traverse of its narrow mile-long crest is a classic and is best reached from the south by an easy screeshoot. The usual approach path, from the coast at Inverkirkaig, can be continued eastward to Elphin.

Except as a viewpoint, Canisp (2779 feet) is disappointing, but across lovely Loch Assynt rises Quinag (2653 feet), a five-topped massif bold as a clenched fist, each knuckle a great rock buttress. It is the final mountain of Torridonian sandstone and is especially imposing seen from Kylesku ferry. The summit crest is most easily gained by the gentle south-east ridge from the A894 above Skiag Bridge.

Eastwards the remote mysterious massif of Ben More Assynt (3273 feet) hides its ten tops behind lesser shoulders. The complete traverse of its ridges is an excellent expedition of some 25 miles, but the going is rough, rocky, and exposed and some scrambling is involved. Below the northern summit the Eas Coulin Falls plunge some 400 feet towards the head of Loch Glencoul.

Reay

Outstanding among other shapely but lesser peaks behind Cape Wrath is Foinaven (2980 feet) whose white screes and high cliffs support a complex of rocky ridges. The traverse of Foinaven and nearby Arkle (2580 feet) from Gualin House to Loch Stack Lodge on the A838 is a magnificent journey.

Finally, Ben Hope (3040 feet) and Ben Loyal (2504 feet) rise either side of the sea loch of the Kyle of Tongue. The latter is an especially attractive peak dubbed 'Queen of Scottish Mountains'. The panorama from its five granite tops extends to Orkney and their traverse makes a fine ridge walk.

Climbing Information

Few concentrations of rock-climbing, although a few routes are scattered among the rugged peaks. Good snow/ice conditions are infrequent. **Summer** rock-climbs exist on the steep **Torridonian sandstone** buttresses at W. ends of such celebrated peaks as **Suilven** and **Stac Pollaidh** and on NE. or 'Barrel Buttress' (215 300) of **Quinag**: good **winter** climbs have also been made among the gullies of the long W. face of this mountain. Famed in climbing circles are the 1000-ft routes on the N. buttress and NE. face of **Sgurr an Fhidhleir** (095 055) of Ben More Coigach. Only notable concentration of **summer** climbing is on:
Foinaven: a complex mountain with several large cliffs among the corries and ridges of its N. flank. Best known: **Creag Urbhard** (or 'Dionard') (348 490): NE.-facing **quartzite** cliff nearly a mile long with over 20 recorded routes to date, up to 1000 ft in length (much exploratory scope). A very remote cliff in a wild situation.

Sea-cliffs and Heritage Coast

It would be fair to say that most Britons feel an affinity with the sea, and in fact no country in the world has a stronger maritime heritage. This partly explains the magnetic pull of coastal walking, which is statistically the most popular of pedestrian pleasures. Those walking a stretch of the Cornish cliffs (preferably in winter), when the surf is crashing, the spume flying, and the clouds racing, can still detect an air redolent of tall ships and daring exploits.

Nostalgia apart, our coast is one of the most varied, and most beautiful, in the world. Avaricious spoliation has largely been halted, thanks to enlightened awareness and preservation schemes like Enterprise Neptune. Conservation together with accessibility are the two prongs of the current programme. Thus the leisure-walker now has a choice of coastline on which he may roam legally, that earlier generations could only have dreamed about.

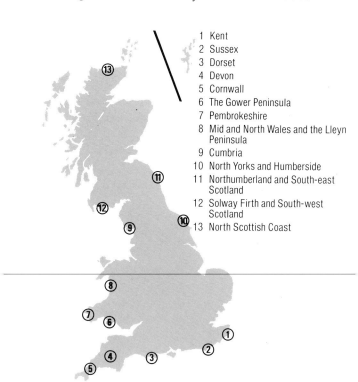

1 Kent
2 Sussex
3 Dorset
4 Devon
5 Cornwall
6 The Gower Peninsula
7 Pembrokeshire
8 Mid and North Wales and the Lleyn Peninsula
9 Cumbria
10 North Yorks and Humberside
11 Northumberland and South-east Scotland
12 Solway Firth and South-west Scotland
13 North Scottish Coast

As just one example, the entire West Country coast from Poole Harbour to Minehead in Somerset is now traced by a continuous path of 515 miles. The network of established paths is so widespread that almost every section of coast which has been designated as being of particular natural beauty may be explored by walkers.

Above all, this includes coastal high country where rolling hills or towering cliffs form splendid bastions against the incoming sea. Cliff-walking in remote areas of Britain means escape from cars, concrete, and crowds. The benefits include distant seascape horizons, invigorating air, exercise to stimulate the circulation, and the chance to enjoy nature relatively undisturbed where land and sea meet.

Practical Points

● Knowledge of sea-cliff walking comes with experience. One soon learns that wet chalk can be very slippery; that farmers sometimes fence dangerously close to cliff-tops edged by public paths (if in doubt trespass); that gullies littered with shale and loose boulders require careful traversing. Start modestly, progress safely.

● The dangers of walking too close to cliff edges are obvious but often ignored. Subsidence after prolonged wet weather, fierce windy gusts across exposed headlands, or simply overgrowth which hides a cliff fissure are all hazards, and can be fatal.

● Beach-walking over smooth sand may appear distinctly attractive from a high-level viewpoint, especially if the cliff-top path is rough and undulating. Before scrambling down, consider the prospect of being cut off below an unclimbable overhang by an incoming tide – a very common occurrence.

● On the credit side, coastal walking presents few navigation problems. But do not dispense with large-scale maps or compass. Obligatory deviations for towns, army ranges, landslips, etc. may be necessary. Detours via country lanes, farm fields, or open country can be intricate and lengthy even with direction aids.

● Coastal routes can be very strenuous, particularly for novice walkers. Unlike tarmac roads – so smooth and blandly graded – footpaths follow natural contours. Any succession of switch-back ups and downs can be tiring and time-consuming to negotiate. Consider those map contours carefully and set prospective mileage well within personal capability.

● Some coasts are well endowed with facilities, notably holiday resort strips in high summer. Along others, like West Wales, Northumberland, or the Western Highlands, there is often a dearth of amenities. Long distances may separate available supplies of food and drink. Self-sufficiency means self-reliance and the burden of extra provisions in the rucksack is worth it. Only backpackers enjoy total independence on long-distance coastal paths.

SEA-CLIFFS AND HERITAGE COAST

Kent

Essential Information

Location and cliff walk: South-east of county between Folkestone and Kingsdown (13 miles)

Distances from main towns: Canterbury 15 miles; Maidstone 35 miles; Medway Towns 50 miles

Suggested bases: Kingsdown, Dover, Folkestone

Access routes: M20/A20 (west); A2 (central); A258 (east)

BR stations: Folkestone, Dover, Martin Mill, Walmer

Youth hostel: Dover

OS map: 179

Looking south-west along the White Cliffs towards Dover Harbour.

For centuries this English county remained essentially rural with urban pockets. Within the short period following the Second World War, however, the picture has been all but reversed. The coast is a ribbon metropolis for the most part now, with the single, splendid exception of the section between Folkestone and Kingsdown which includes the famous White Cliffs. Somehow the precious natural beauty of the South Foreland area has been preserved, notably between the village of Kingsdown and the ancient Cinque Port of Dover. Expansion of the harbour complex, clusters of signal pylons, new roads, and debris of old wartime defences may have scarred but they have certainly not obliterated the timeless majesty of the chalk cliffs. Perhaps we are fortunately now conservation-

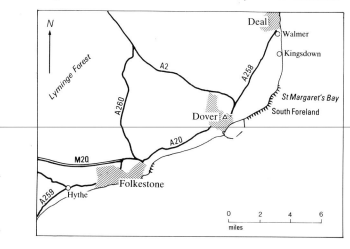

conscious enough to ensure it never will be.

The natural splendour crossed by this 13-mile path above the English Channel is only half the attraction. For it is also a walk through 2000 years of history; a unique pedestrian route with nothing quite comparable anywhere else in these islands. A combination with high appeal for all who enjoy leisure-walking.

For those completing the marathon North Downs Way, Dover is the ultimate objective. As the walker approaches via the rounded green hills above Folkestone and follows the cliff-tops above the town to the end of the Way on the Western Heights above Dover, it might be thought that the path is crossing the most spectacular heights, but there are yet more to come. Dover itself is dominated by its mighty castle which stands above the town and harbour on a high hill.

There is easy walking east-wards from Dover along an unmistakable path, past the marked spot where Blériot landed after flying the Channel in 1909, past evocative remnants of wartime pill-boxes, the lighthouse where Marconi once experimented with wireless, the Churchill Memorial Park, and the Dover Patrol look-out point above St Margaret's Bay, itself the departure point for countless Channel swimmers since the first, Mathew Webb, in 1875.

Greensward walking of the best kind follows, with magnificent seascapes and France tantalizingly close on a clear day. The path swoops from 400 feet to sea-level just before Kingsdown. A necessary note of caution must be sounded: deep fissures encroach close to the path in one or two places, and walkers starting from Kingsdown should not walk below the cliffs at low tide.

Climbing Information
Sea-cliff Climbing

Much of Britain's coastline, particularly in the south and west, is cliff-girt and provides rock-climbing, often of superlative quality. Typically the weather is better than it is in the mountains, and as few cliffs are far from a road, such climbing is very popular.

However, sea-cliffs are serious places. The sea is dangerous and climbers have been drowned. There is usually no easy escape downwards from a climb, for safety is at the top! Indeed, the Sea Cliff Traverse – the crossing of perhaps hundreds of yards of cliff, bottoming in deep water and from which upward escape is impossible – is a real expedition involving commitment and hazards of a style encountered usually only on large mountains.

Within a few feet of the sea, almost any rock (even chalk) is solid enough to be climbed, but even the best rock is liable to be loose, earthy, and dangerous at the cliff top. Most sea-cliffs are for experienced climbers only, although there are notable exceptions.

Unlike mountain areas, rock-climbing is often misunderstood by the local people and authorities at the seaside. Sometimes capable and responsible climbers may be equated with the more usual stranded tourists: such situations must be tactfully handled. By agreement with the B.M.C., certain cliffs are closed during the nesting of rare seabirds: such restrictions should be respected.

Because there are thousands of climbs at hundreds of locations, and because new areas are constantly being discovered, only the major recognized climbing areas are mentioned here.

Sussex

Essential Information

Locations and cliff walks: East of Hastings (5 miles); west of Eastbourne (10 miles)

Distances from main towns: Hastings 2 miles; Eastbourne 2 miles; Brighton 14 miles; London 60 miles

Suggested bases: Hastings, Eastbourne, Fairlight, Seaford

Access routes: Off A259 north-east of Hastings, west of Eastbourne

BR stations: Eastbourne, Hastings, Guestling Green

Youth hostels: Guestling, Beachy Head, Alfriston

OS map: 199

Hastings section

One famous stretch of Heritage Coast graces the Sussex sea-board, as well as a section in the care of the National Trust, not quite so well known but delightfully attractive. Fairlight Glen is sufficiently off the beaten track to enjoy relative seclusion; it is reached via the minor road which leads off the A259 for Pett and the aptly named Cliff End.

The pedestrian route is somewhat obscure at first, but those heading for Hastings will soon discover the cliff-top path. Walkers tramping these 400-foot sandstone cliffs for the first time will be agreeably surprised at the vistas which this sudden (and often unsuspec-

ted) elevation provides, over Romney Marsh and Dungeness Point.

There is habitation around Fairlight Cove, but it is a casual, rough-road enclave, pleasant enough to walk through en route to the three deep, wooded combes or glens that give the area its name. The area is quite reminiscent of Scotland in places, a riot of gorse in summer, with luxuriant south-facing defiles fed by streams. The path gives splendid views over Hastings and beyond on approach, eventually descending East Hill to the Old Town. This is still tinged with an Elizabethan air and is by far the most picturesque quarter of this second Cinque Port.

Eastbourne section

From Eastbourne, at the beginning of the South Downs Way, starts one of the most frequently tramped cliff paths in Britain; beyond Birling Gap, however, serious walkers will enter far quieter terrain. On high days and holidays the heights above Beachy Head are thronged with milling sight-seers. In summer, it is prudent to arrive in the early morning; cars are best parked at the western edge of East-

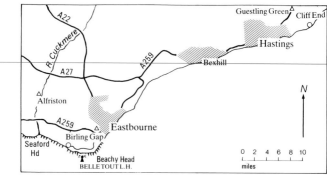

bourne. From here, there is ascent by footpath to the headland at 534 feet.

From the summit of this majestic chalk bluff, the lighthouse far below seems toy-like and it is not difficult to imagine why Lovers' Leap is so named. The green turf pathway and the western prospect of the Seven Sisters cliffs is even more alluring to walkers, undulating voluptuously beyond the old Belle Tout lighthouse. The contrast between crowded Beachy Head and the green-velvet peace of the roller-coaster Seven Sisters is total. This is still old-world Sussex, a quiet corner of England suspended between sky and sea, each rapid rise and fall of greensward known individually by generations of shepherds, as they knew each member of their flocks: Baily Hill, Flagstaff, Rough Brow, Haven Brow.

The most westerly of the downland undulations swoops downhill to Cuckmere Haven to rejoin the tarmac, noise, and fumes of the contemporary south-coast scene, but the pleasure is not quite over. The mile-long detour inland, following the South Downs Way, enables the walker to cross the river and return seawards. For on the western side is Seaford Head, yet another dazzling white dome above the promenade of Seaford, the last of the Sussex chalk cliffs.

The chalk cliffs of Beachy Head.

Dorset

Essential Information

Locations and cliff walks: Purbeck Hills (east) (20 miles); Chesil Bank to Charmouth (west) (15 miles)

Distances from main towns: Weymouth 4 miles; Dorchester 7 miles; Bournemouth 17 miles

Suggested bases: Charmouth, Weymouth, Swanage, West Bay (Bridport)

Access routes: A351 (east) Swanage; A352/A353 (central), between Weymouth and Wareham; A35/B3157 (west), between Charmouth and Abbotsbury

BR stations: Weymouth, Wareham

Youth hostels: Litton Cheney, Bridport, Swanage, Lulworth Cove

OS maps: 194, 195

Purbeck Hills section

There are 35 miles of elevated beauty along the Dorset coastline; even the sea-level sections are fascinating around Chesil Bank and Portland Bill. For the walker this is among the best of British coastlines. West of Poole Harbour the linear sprawl of urban development, which is effectively continuous from far-off Newhaven, ends abruptly. Beyond, along the pedestrian route, lies an English landscape still miraculously intact, with strong nineteenth-century overtones.

The delight begins with the visual feast of Corfe Castle, appropriately built in Purbeck stone, and the village which still retains a medieval appearance. The surroundings of splendid green hills dotted with old stone quarries form the unique Isle of Purbeck. South of Swanage extend the limestone cliffs, shot through with Purbeck marble, the stone once sought so eagerly. Tilly Whim Caves testify to past industry, as do the now-deserted burrowings around Dancing Ledge and East Man. A dramatic cliff-top walk between Durlston Head and the tiny twelfth-century chapel which stands isolated on St Aldhelm's Head becomes even more spectacular westwards. The route takes in the secluded Chapman's Pool, the tumbled rock and shale chaos of Kimmeridge Ledges, the exquisite formation of Lulworth Cove. The latter is approached by a path winding 500 feet above sea-level in places, swooping to the foreshore in others. The section between Kimmeridge and Lulworth is closed occasionally for army exercises but is open most of the year.

A blend of limestone and chalk cliffs continue, punctuated by eroded outcrops like Durdle Door arch, the path undulating over glorious open heights and culminating with White Nothe cliff, 500 feet above the tiny hamlet of Osmington Mills, snug in its deep wooded combe. There are magnificent views extending far over Weymouth and Portland Bill.

Chesil Bank section

Abbotsbury epitomizes rural Dorset physically and aesthetically, a settlement of thatch and golden stone of eleventh-century origins beautifully proportioned and in a very attractive setting. The massive fifteenth-century Monks Barn, the lonely hill-top St Catherine's Chapel, and the historic Swannery: these are just three gems at the head of the lagoon which is known as The Fleet, walled by the shingle of Chesil Bank.

The cliffs rise once more beyond Burton Bradstock, a series of sandstone faces split massively by lateral defiles like those of West Bay, Eype Mouth, and Seatown. Although visitors flock here in vast numbers in the summer months, they are not over crowded, while the heights in between are scarcely explored, despite the well-defined roller-coaster path which traces the coastline.

This is a magnificent walk (a section of the South-West Peninsula Coast Path), culminating with Golden Cap, the highest cliff on the south coast, a regal bluff soaring to 625 feet and literally capped with gold sandstone which glints richly in sunlight. Majestic sweeping panoramic views of Lyme Bay and the Devon hills stretching out beyond are revealed from these summits.

The subsequent descent of Timber Hill to Charmouth is tackled with a sense of achievement by most walkers, since it is a muscle-testing route in places. The 400-foot-high Black Ven is the final peak which separates Charmouth from Lyme Regis and the Devon border.

Durdle Door, west of Lulworth Cove.

Climbing Information

An important climbing coast, not least because of proximity to London and population centres of the South. Rock usually excellent yellow **jurassic limestone** ('Purbeck' and 'Portland Stone'). Best areas:

● **Swanage:** some 4 m. of almost continuous S.-facing cliffs extend from Anvil Point (030 769) westward to St Aldhelm's Head. Over 500 climbs recorded near most of the accessible points, typically vertical and up to 120 ft in height (all grades, but few easy, and all in a potentially serious situation). A very atmospheric place.

● **Lulworth:** the limestone outcrops to the sea again E. and W. of Lulworth Cove (826 797). Over a dozen climbs up to 170 ft have been made between the Cove and Stair Hole while eastward the cliffs provide a classic traverse of 1 mile to Mupe Bay; straightforward climbing but not to be undertaken lightly.

● **Portland:** several dozen short and technical climbs up to 60 ft max. (none easy) have been recorded on the East Cliff at G.R. 691 697.

Devon

Essential Information

Locations and cliff walks: South Devon: Lyme Regis to Sidmouth (19 miles); Torcross to Plymouth Sound (33 miles). North Devon: Countisbury to Combe Martin Bay (18 miles); Westward Ho! to Welcombe Bay (22 miles)

Distances from main towns: South: Exeter 12 miles; Torquay 16 miles. North: Minehead 12 miles; Bideford 4 miles

Suggested bases: Sidmouth, Salcombe, Lynmouth, Bude

Access routes: South: A3052 between Lyme Regis and Sidmouth; off A379 between Plymouth and Torcross. North: A39/A399 between County Gate and Combe Martin; A39 between Bideford and Bude

BR stations: Axminster, Plymouth, Minehead, Bideford

Youth hostels: South: Beer, Salcombe, Bigbury-on-Sea. North: Lynton, Hartland

OS maps: 180, 190, 192, 193, 202

South Devon

Above Lyme Regis is the famous 'landslip', a 5-mile ridge path forming a rugged divide between the chalk and underlying clay.

Across the River Axe, the chalk cliffs of Beer Head rise almost out of character with the red-earth landscape of Devon. A section of coast path begins above the harbour and continues as a bridleway to Sidmouth. In between are fine open cliffs close to 500 feet high.

Sidmouth is sedate, while Peak Hill is one of Devon's most spectacular red sandstone heights. The cliff path gives views across Torbay.

Torcross at the western end of Slapton Ley is battered by gales but none the less beauti-

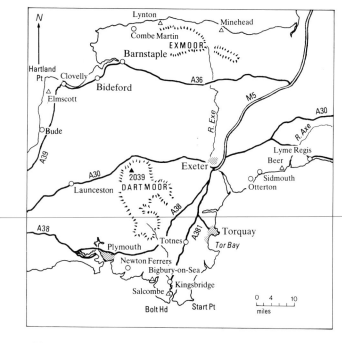

ful. It is a hard haul to Start Point but this is arguably the best part of the coast, unblemished by roads from here to Salcombe.

Within the cliff-girt Kings-bridge estuary a ferry plies from East Portlemouth to Salcombe; the next section from Bolt Head to Bolt Tail is memorable. The terrain is massively rugged, rising to some 400 feet.

Westwards the path becomes fragmented but beyond Mothercombe is another fine stretch across Beacon Hill to Noss Mayo and Newton Ferrers where a ferry plies to Warren Point. From here the path makes a dramatic traverse above Wembury Bay.

North Devon

North Devon differs in geology and climate from the southern coast. Atlantic breakers batter the western seaboard and bare grey cliffs of metamorphic culms and shales predominate. Initially, though, west of the Somerset border the heights of Exmoor are heather-clad and cut by wooded combes.

The coastal path is well defined and much walked but involves steep ascents and descents. There is natural drama at almost every turn from County Gate to Combe Martin.

From Westward Ho! there is rugged beauty on the path to Clovelly. Around Bideford Bay, the tiny hamlet of Bucks Mills may impress more than Clovelly, now, sadly, over-commercialized.

There is more rough walking in places, some precipitous ups and downs, and patches of heavy overgrowth. Stark breath-taking beauty awaits around Hartland Point, a stern coastline of jagged reefs and towering cliffs.

Climbing Information
South Devon

West of the Exe much of the coast is rocky and climbs have been made along most of it.

Torbay

Devonian limestone forms the headlands of Hopes Nose and Berry Head. Each holds several cliffs with excellent climbing and traverses. Best are:

● **Ansteys Cove/Long Quarry Point** (937 651) and adjoining cliffs: more than 60 climbs (all grades and types) up to 400 ft, mostly 100–200 ft. Some less serious.

● **Daddyhole Cliff** (926 627) and adjoining crags: some 50 climbs up to 190 ft but mostly shorter (all grades). Only the Main Cliff rises from the sea; all can be reached at high tide.

● **Berry Head** (947 567): several cliffs and quarries round the headland hold over 50 climbs, from 50 ft VD to 220 ft HVS. Also traverses.

● **The Old Redoubt** (942 562) close by, awesome overhanging 250-ft cliff rises from deep water: its base can only be reached below mid-tide. A series of classic hard climbs and two famous traverses.

North Devon

Many high and dramatic cliffs but composed of a wide variety of sedimentary rocks typically untrustworthy and often awful. Best climbs:

● **Lundy Island**: 12 m. off Hartland Point. Over 150 climbs on rough red **granite**, most on wild W. coast, some 3 m. of continuous cliff. All standards up to XS; longest 390 ft.

● **Baggy Point** (419 406): a much indented and complex headland of **old red sandstone** some 9 m. NW. of Barnstaple. More than 30 climbs, principally on slabs, some quite steep and up to 320 ft in height. Grades from VD–XS. Cliff bottom sea-washed at high tide.

● **Blackchurch** (299 266): some 2 m. W. of Clovelly, an impressive cliff of **culm** forming steep overlapping slabs and grooves. Over a dozen climbs, all hard (from VS–XS), between 200–270 ft in length.

Cornwall

Essential Information

Locations and cliff walks: South: Land's End to Mousehole (12 miles); Mullion Cove to Coverack (14 miles); Portloe to Mevagissey (10 miles); Polkerris to Polperro (10 miles). North: Marsland Mouth to Tintagel (18 miles); Port Isaac to Pentire Point (6 miles); Trevose Head to Newquay (9 miles); St Agnes Head to Godrevy Point (10 miles); St Ives to Gurnard's Head (6 miles)

Distances from main towns: South: Penzance 10 miles; Falmouth 10 miles; St Austell 5 miles; Plymouth 20 miles. North: Bude 1 mile; Launceston 17 miles; Newquay 2 miles; Penzance 8 miles

Suggested bases: South: St Just, Porthleven, St Mawes, Mevagissey, Fowey.

North: Bude, Tintagel, Newquay, St Ives

Access routes: South: Off A38 between Liskeard and Bodmin; B3723 south from St Austell; A3078 between Tregony and St Mawes; A394 between Marazion and Helston; A30 between Penzance and Land's End. North: Off A39 from Devon/Cornwall boundary to Indian Queens; A30 Indian Queens to Hayle; B3306 St Ives to St Just

BR stations: Looe, St Austell, Falmouth, Penzance, Newquay

Youth hostels: Golant, Boswinger, Falmouth, Coverack, Penzance, Land's End, Perranporth, Treyarnon Bay, Tintagel, Boscastle

OS maps: 190, 200, 201, 203, 204

The Cornish peninsula is formed of Devonian rock with massive granite intrusions. Inlets and headlands included, the coast extends for 250 miles.

South Cornwall

Although Land's End has been marred by development, the walker has access to natural grandeur, notably to Gwennap Head.

The Lizard Peninsula is a geological intrusion of igneous serpentine; the most impressive stretch is south of Mullion Cove, and Kynance Cove is strikingly beautiful. Around the headland lie Cadgwith and the chasm of the Devil's Frying Pan. The going is hard around Black Head to Coverack.

The Roseland Peninsula is fertile and temperate. From

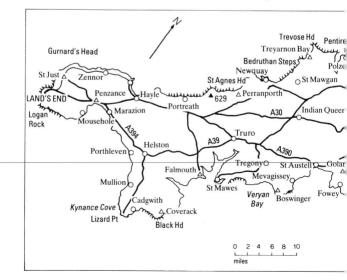

Portloe the path is exhilarating in either direction; north around Veryan Bay to Dodman Point it is memorable. Beyond Par Sands the path winds from Polkerris around Gribbin Head, via Fowey, to Polruan; 6 hard miles follow to Polperro.

North Cornwall

The river combe at Marsland Mouth forms the county boundary. With hardly a break in elevated beauty the path winds past High Cliff (732 feet), the loftiest headland in England. The dramatic surroundings increase between Boscastle Harbour and Tintagel Head.

From Port Isaac there is green and glorious walking to Pentire Point via Port Quin. A series of headlands and fissured cliffs give way to the holiday beaches of Polzeath. There is fine cliff-top walking between Trevose Head and Newquay, especially above Bedruthan Steps.

South-west the path skirts St Agnes Beacon (629 feet), 5 miles beyond Perranporth Sands, to begin another cliff traverse. Past Portreath it becomes awesome above Deadman's Cove and Hell's Mouth, below 250-foot-high cliffs.

From St Ives to Gurnard's Head the path is little walked. Here tower fierce cliffs, rising to 300 or 400 feet in places.

Climbing Information

The rough red **granite** of the Land's End Peninsula was the birthplace of sea-cliff climbing. Climbs from St Ives to Penzance; major concentrations at:

● **Bosigran** (416 369): 4 m. NE. of St Just. Over 70 climbs on SW.-facing Main Face and adjoining facets. From D to XS, many in middle grades and up to 220 ft in height. Easy access along grass ledge above sea. More straightforward routes on **Porthmoina Island** in cove beneath, access at low tide; also on arete on SW. side of cove. Beyond at G.R. 415 366 is **Great Zawn**, containing most concentrated series of hard climbs in SW., 21 steep and superb routes around 200 ft in height.

● **Pedn-Men-Du** (347 263): line of cliffs 400 yds W. of Sennen. Some 50 climbs, steep but mostly easy or middle grades, around 70–80 ft high. Easy virtually tide-free access.

● **Chair Ladder** (365 216): 2½ m. S. of Land's End roadhead. A series of steep buttresses with prominent horizontal faulting rise from sea, bases sea-washed until half-tide. Over 40 climbs up to 200 ft (many middle grades). Pleasant SW. aspect; popular cliff.

● Other important cliffs: **Land's End** (342 252), **Pordenack Point** (346 243), and **Fox Promontory** (362 224)

● High-quality climbs, mostly modern, mostly very hard, all of extreme seriousness have been made on the less reliable rocks of both N. and S. coasts further east. Notable: **Pentire Head** (924 805), **Cligga Head** (737 537), and **Carn Gowla** (698 512).

The Gower Peninsula

Essential Information

Locations and cliff walks: Port-Eynon Bay to Worms Head via Rhossili Down (8 miles)
Distances from main towns: Swansea 14 miles
Suggested base: Port-Eynon
Access routes: M4 (north), exit 47; A4118 (east) from Swansea
BR station: Swansea
Youth hostel: Port-Eynon
OS map: 159

Thinly populated with a scattering of hamlets and no towns, the Gower Peninsula is a secluded backwater of Wales, possessing one of Britain's most regal headlands, Worms Head. Its proximity to Swansea means that it is crowded in summer, but in early or late season it is a tranquil haven, in parts outstandingly beautiful.

There are few roads on the peninsula and, indeed, the best way to discover the Gower is on foot. Footpaths cover the whole of the peninsula, running inland over the hills and wooded commons, and tracing virtually the entire coastline of great limestone cliffs.

West of the Mumbles along the southern coast stretch a succession of spectacular high spots: Bacon Hole, Mitchin Hole, Pwll-du Bay. The limestone bluff of Pwll-du Head is the highest point on the Gower coast – 320 feet – and the cliff-

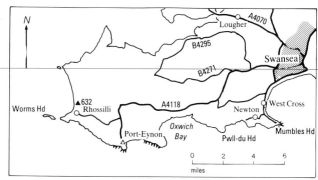

Left: Lewes Castle above Mewslade Bay.
Above: Threecliff Bay.

top path gives splendid views across the Bristol Channel. Further west lies Threecliff Bay, named for the three limestone crags which bound it on the east; beyond, the bluff of Great Tor dominates Oxwich Bay.

Port-Eynon to Worms Head

Oxwich Bay, half-way along the south coast, is rightly popular with visitors. It is now for the most part a Nature Reserve of wooded cliffs and protected sand-dunes. Two nature trails have been established in the area, revealing the rich and varied flora and fauna.

Round the headland, Port-Eynon is a strategic base from which to explore the most dramatic of the coastal high spots. Near by are caves, cliffs, and inlets: Culver Hole, Paviland Cave, and the cliff-girt Mewslade Bay.

Rhossili Down is the highest point on the peninsula (632 feet); there is a fine walk across the Down to Rhossili village, then by a mile-long path along the cliff-top to the spectacular promontory of Worms Head. The views on approach are truly memorable. The promontory is a welter of chasms, effectively two massive outcrops spanned by the narrow but negotiable natural arch of the Devil's Bridge.

Climbing Information

This S.-facing coast, some 15 miles long, holds many cliffs of **carboniferous** ('mountain') **limestone**. Unlike other limestone sea-cliffs, which typically form a continuous wall, the Gower crags rise individually, each with a character of its own, and often with vertical strata as the ends of great rock folds. The atmosphere is pleasant and, because most of the crags rise from wide tide-washed sandy beaches, lacks the seriousness of e.g. Dorset. Major climbing areas are:

● **Threecliff** (538 878): 6 m. W. of Mumbles Head; a striking mini-mountain-like feature rises from the river-mouth sands and gives a sequence of medium-grade climbs, mostly on slabs, up to 150 ft in length.

● **Great Tor** (530 877): 6½ m. W. of Mumbles Head and **Little Tor** near by, are distinctive pinnacle-like buttresses with steep walls and impressive aretes. Many climbs (all grades), the longest 240 ft.

● **Mewslade** (416 872): 13½ m. W. of Mumbles Head; the most continuous series of cliffs in Gower rise from the sands of this beautiful bay between the impressive castle-like buttresses of Thurba Head and Lewes Castle. Walls, chimneys, cracks, and aretes (all grades), mostly steep, up to 140 ft, as well as short boulder-problem pitches.

135

Pembrokeshire

Essential Information

Locations and cliff walks: Stackpole Quay to St Govan's Head (4 miles); St Ann's Head to Wooltack Point (7 miles); Aber-mawr to Fishguard Bay (11 miles); Dinas Head to Moylgrove (12 miles)

Distances from main towns: Tenby 9 miles; Haverfordwest 12 miles

Suggested bases: Tenby, St David's, Fishguard

Access routes: Off A40 (north and central) between Haverfordwest and Fishguard; A478 (south) between Narberth and Tenby; A487 (west) between St David's and Newport

BR stations: Tenby, Pembroke, Fishguard

Youth hostels: Pentlepoir, Marloes Sands, Broad Haven, St David's, Trevine, Pwll Deri

OS maps: 145, 157, 158

The Pembrokeshire coast is traced for 168 miles by an established long-distance footpath, which offers splendid opportunities for a variety of walking expeditions.

Stackpole Quay to St Govan's Head

From tiny Stackpole Quay, the path traverses spectacular wild cliffs around Stackpole Head, culminating with St Govan's Head and the twin limestone pinnacles of Elegug Stacks. The cliff-faces plummet sheer and in wild weather the scene is awesomely beautiful. Care is needed in the vicinity of the Devil's Punch Bowl, a 150-foot chasm. A Ministry of Defence

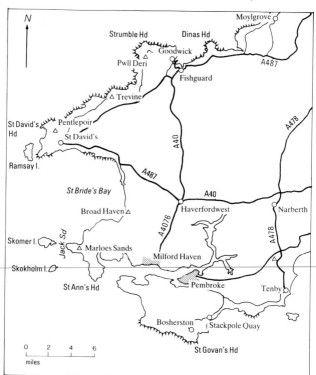

complex makes an inland detour obligatory on occasion, via the hamlet of Bosherston.

St Ann's Head to Wooltack Point

Almost as exciting is the section of path beyond Milford Haven, which links St Ann's Head and Wooltack Point. West from the lighthouse and road (accessible by car), the cliffs quickly become free of people and increasingly grand of aspect. The offshore islands of Gateholm, Skomer, and Skokholm add drama; this is a protected domain of seabirds and seals.

Aber-mawr to Fishguard Bay

St David's Head is the craggiest promontory at Ramsay Sound, but for dramatic cliffs Strumble Head is superior. Walk the coast path north from Abermawr for proof; here are grand fissured cliffs above pounding surf, the tops marked with prehistoric remains. The path itself is rough and devious, but highly rewarding. Only the strongest walkers will wish to complete this rough coast route in one stint to Fishguard harbour. The going is tough almost all the way to Goodwick.

Dinas Head to Moylgrove

Old Fishguard is full of character, the deep-water harbour snugly picturesque. There is an easy ascent (at first alongside the road), north-east to Dinas Head, with magnificent views back across the bay, the path flirting with cliff edges and then circumnavigating the prominent headland. For lovers of lonely coastlines, there are more fine cliffs north of Newport village. From here a very secluded stretch of path leads past Moylgrove.

Climbing Information

This has become one of the most important sea-cliff climbing areas. Miles of **carboniferous limestone** cliffs face S. to the Bristol Channel, while rocks and crags of very different character and structure wall St Bride's and Cardigan Bays.

● **Lydstep** (092 975): 3 m. SW. of Tenby. Nearly 1 m. of cliff extends W. towards Old Castle Head. Often vertically bedded, giving face and crack climbing on steep smooth walls. Most are tidal with caves and arches at sea-level. Many climbs (harder grades to XS), up to 150 ft.

● **Stackpole Head/Mowing Ward** (995 943): 4½ m. S. of Pembroke. A line of continuous cliff forms twin headlands of stark horizontally bedded and unusually sound rock rising some 130 ft above the sea. The base is tidal and the cliff-top flat. Hard and generally serious climbs.

● **St Govan's Head** area (975 928): 5½ m. S. of Pembroke; similar to Stackpole Head but rock ledges give easier access at sea-level and cliff is more broken. Many good climbs (mostly hard, few easier), up to 130 ft.

● **Flimston** area (930 945): 5½ m. SW. of Pembroke. Similar to Stackpole and St Govan's but the higher cliffs (150 ft) tend to be looser. Hard climbs at Bullslaughter Bay, and the twin Elugug Stacks offer most unusual ascents.

Interesting climbs and traverses have been made on Marloes Peninsula and in St Bride's Bay; other area of concentrated climbing:

● **St David's Head** (722 280): 2½ m. NW. of St David's. Nearly a mile of NW.-facing coastline holds cliffs some 200 ft high rising from deep water and screened from above by steep convex gorse-covered slopes. The rock is **gabbro**. Four main cliffs, separated by deep inlets, form a series of buttresses and walls giving many climbs of good quality (all grades from D to XS), some as long as 320 ft. Similar rock on adjacent island of **Ramsey** gives fine climbs up to 400 ft.

Mid and North Wales and the Lleyn Peninsula

Essential Information

Locations and cliff walks: North Wales: Gwbert-on-Sea to Aberporth (8 miles); vicinity of Aberystwyth and Newquay. Lleyn Peninsula: Hell's Mouth to Aberdaron Bay (7 miles); St Mary's Church to Morfa Nefyn (15 miles)

Distances from main towns: Cardigan 3 miles; Aberystwyth 1 mile; Pwllheli 8 miles

Access routes: Off A487 between Cardigan and Aberystwyth; A497 between Criccieth and Nefyn; B4413 and B4417 between Aberdaron and Llithfaen

BR stations: Aberystwyth, Pwllheli

Youth hostels: Poppit Sands, Newquay, Borth

OS maps: 115, 116, 123

Mid and North Wales

There are numerous stretches of the Cardigan Bay coast worthy of exploration between Cardigan town and Aberyst-wyth. From Gwbert-on-Sea, north of Cardigan, there is a lovely lowish cliff section to Aberporth some 8 miles distant. Just one minor road intersects the seclusion at the halfway mark, Mwynt.

Newquay is a popular but compact resort, much favoured by small-boat sailors. The surroundings are attractive, especially the headland protecting the harbour. The cliffs are perforated with caves, and there are splendid views from Newquay Head, 300 feet above sea-level. The stiff path from Llangranog to the point of Ynys-Lochtyn, one mile seaward between Aberporth and Newquay, is one of rugged surprises too.

Aberystwyth also offers fine high-level pedestrian routes, both north and south of its

138

pleasant estuary setting. To the south, Pen Dinas boasts a great Iron Age fort on the 414-foot-high summit, accessible from an easy path near the town's touring site. White Cliff, high above the River Ystwyth, is another imposing objective, reached by a short walk. To the north, Constitution Hill rises to 485 feet, giving views across the great bay westwards and over the mighty Plynlimon range inland.

The Lleyn Peninsula

Thrusting into the Atlantic, the Lleyn Peninsula is understandably dubbed the Land's End of Wales. There is good and varied coast walking on this 25-mile-long promontory of rocky headlands, mainly around the southern tip and on the western flank below Morfa Nefyn.

From the south-facing storm-beach of Porth Neigwl (Hell's Mouth) there is comparatively gentle walking at first, with the scene increasing in rugged grandeur above Bardsey Sound and the off-shore island, to majestic sea-lashed precipices now protected by the National Trust. The wild beauty of the coast continues, virtually unbroken, to Morfa Nefyn.

Beyond here, Nant Gwytheyrn (Vortigern's Valley) and the three-headed summits of Yr Eifl (The Rivals; 1850 feet), slightly inland, are just two of the accredited high spots; the latter, in particular, providing views right across the Island of Anglesey. This is a lovely area of Wales, remaining relatively untrodden away from the holiday strip between Pwllheli and Abersoch, dotted with seabird sanctuaries and off-shore seal colonies.

Bardsey Island (Ynys Enlli).

Climbing Information

Surprisingly few good sea-cliffs. The most notable exceptions are on Anglesey and:

● **Great Orme** immediately NW. (1 + mile) of Llandudno. A big headland of **carboniferous limestone** holds a vast amount of rock but the best climbing is concentrated on six crags outcropping from the grassy hillsides and not actually rising from the sea. Climbs are VS or harder, and from 90–180 ft, the rock is sometimes poor. Best is on St Tudno's Buttress (G.R. 754 843) with a dozen climbs in superb situation.

● **Little Orme** (815 825): 2 m. E. of Llandudno; a complex and extremely serious cliff of **carboniferous limestone** holding several faces and often with difficult access – typically swimming or abseil. Many climbs, all in hard grades generally XS, ranging from 120 ft to 640 ft in height. Some routes demand aid techniques and bivouacs are not unknown. A playground for hard climbers only. Some climbs exist at **Cilan** (294 234) near Abersoch and **Nefyn** (318 422) 5 m. NW. of Pwllheli (all hard). Easier and longer routes on the NW. face of Yr Eifl (351 457) 6 m. N. of Pwllheli, but this is really a mountain crag rising above the sea.

Cumbria

Essential Information

Locations and cliff walks: Arnside,
Morecambe Bay, St Bees Head,
Maryport

Distances from main towns: Morecambe 11 miles; Whitehaven 2 miles

Access routes: M6 (exit 35) and A6 at
Carnforth; A595 and B5345 south of
Whitehaven; A594 Maryport

BR stations: Arnside, St Bees, Maryport

Youth hostels: Arnside, Cockermouth

OS maps: 89, 96, 97

It might be assumed that
Cumbria, the county which
holds England's most majestic
mountains, would have a coastline to match. Yet this is not so
in scenic terms, nor has it been
particularly enhanced by man.
The coast from Morecambe
Sands to Solway Firth represents a ribbon development,
showing the marks of a legacy
of quarrying and heavy industry; a newer, alien complex
called Windscale; and near-
continuous foreshore encroach-
ment by road and railway. Yet
while there are certainly ugly
scars, the coast is none the less
far from dull and does have
one or two quite delightful
stretches which compete with
the outstanding grandeur of
the hinterland.

Arnside and Morecambe Bay

Arnside is one, on the new
southern boundary of Cum-
bria, almost centrally located in
Morecambe Bay. An intriguing
mixture of wilderness and
frenetic holiday bustle per-
vades this vast sea inlet where
the tides recede to infinity.
There is still a public right of
way across the great mud-flats
from Morecambe to Grange-
over-Sands, but it should only
be walked with a knowledge-
able guide. It is the 500-foot-
high Arnside Knott that
primarily appeals to walkers.
The cliff walks and wooded
park are very attractive and
diversely scenic. There is a 2½-
mile nature trail about a mile
south of the little town and
another from the picturesque
Grange-over-Sands (on the
opposite side of the estuary).
The latter winds over Hamps-
fell, a 727-foot limestone scarp,
giving marvellous panoramas
across the Lakeland peaks.

St Bees Head

St Bees Head, the westernmost
headland of Cumbria, is skirted
by road and rail, leaving some
4 miles of red sandstone cliffs
for the seabirds and leisure-
walkers. St Bees is a small resort
with a fine beach below the
cliffs, while Whitehaven at the
northern end of the headland
is industrial though sadly
depressed.

Maryport

Maryport, further north along
the coast, was once important
as a coaling station and iron-
works, but has now partly
assumed the mantle of a resort,
and the once-busy harbour
shelters only leisure craft. To
the north of the old harbour

The red sandstone cliffs of St Bees Head.

stretches an impressive line of low cliffs called the Sea Brows, which was once the site of a Roman settlement. The path traces a route along and below the sandstone bluffs to give an interesting viewpoint across the Solway Firth at its widest and the chance to see a variety of foreshore bird-life.

Climbing Information

St Bees Head (940 140): 3½ m. SW. of Whitehaven, provides the only steep rock on this coast. Horizontally bedded **new red sandstone** forms nearly 2 m. of continuous SW.-facing cliff, broken only once. The rock is vertical and assumes bold features – towers, roofs, and fierce crack-lines – giving a series of hard climbs around 200 ft in height. The cliff bottom is passable at low tide.

141

North Yorks and Humberside

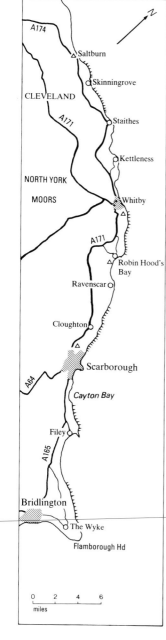

A174
Saltburn
Skinningrove
CLEVELAND
A171
Staithes
Kettleness
NORTH YORK
MOORS
Whitby
A171
Robin Hood's
Bay
Ravenscar
Cloughton
Scarborough
A64
Cayton Bay
Filey
A165
Bridlington
The Wyke
Flamborough Hd

0 2 4 6
miles

Essential Information

Locations and cliff walks: Saltburn to Filey Brigg via Cleveland Way (50 miles); Flamborough Head (4 miles)
Distances from main towns: Scarborough 1 mile; Bridlington 2 miles; York 37 miles
Access routes: Off A165 and 171 between Bridlington and Saltburn
BR stations: Saltburn, Whitby, Scarborough, Filey, Bridlington
Youth hostels: Scarborough, Boggle Hole, Whitby, Saltburn
OS maps: 93, 94, 101

Saltburn to Whitby

The coastal length of the Cleveland Way, rugged and richly atmospheric, is also most visually stimulating, as those who have ever walked south from Saltburn will know. Transformed from remote fishing village to a solid Teesside resort (following Scarborough's renaissance as a spa in the eighteenth century), Saltburn is overshadowed by mighty Hunt Cliff. To the south, the path drops into the defile of Skinningrove, a desolate industrial graveyard in a landscape of dignified grandeur.

From here the route climbs to cross the Cleveland–Yorkshire boundary and ascends the massive 660-foot-high Boulby Cliff. It too is scarred by past exploitation, though this is largely healed by time and nature. Only strong and adventurous walkers tramp these heights, which are truly regal, especially on the approach to Staithes, occupying a quite precipitous cliff defile. It is an exciting path, and not a little tricky in places. Care is needed along the more serrated sections and across Kettleness headland before the descent to magnificent Whitby. This is a port with few equals in

Above: The coast at Whitby.
Below: Dunsley Bay.

the British Isles and none more dramatic in setting, or richer in legacies of seafaring past. (Distance from Saltburn to Whitby 20 miles.)

Whitby to Scarborough

South, the cliffs rise again and no roads encroach on the seaward side until Robin Hood's Bay, 8 miles away. Tough going again if the wind is piping, though glorious if the sun is shining, even though the old smuggler's haunt is now overwhelmed with car-borne crowds. Around the bay, Ravenscar is a favoured walker's watering hole, only slightly commercialized. From here to Scarborough the coastal beauty continues, varying only from outstanding to breath-taking, especially between Robin Hood's Bay and Cloughton Wyke. Impressively rock-girt, Scarborough is bracing, brash, but above all a friendly place. There is fine walking virtually within the town environs and notably towards Filey around Cayton Bay and The Wyke. Chalets and caravans mushroom as the high cliffs recede and the black rock finger of Filey Brigg denotes the end of the long-

distance path, 8 miles from Scarborough. (Distance from Whitby to Scarborough 22 miles.)

Flamborough Head

Like the vicinity of Filey, Flamborough Head in Humberside has its share of holiday camps and tourist development, but there is also the 3-mile Dane's Dyke which bisects the headland. Seawards of Flamborough village from Sewerby stretch 4 miles of cliffs which run outwards to the lighthouse on the wind-swept point. Rising to nearly 400 feet in places, this remote headland is a haven for seabirds including Gannets, Guillemots, and Puffins, which seasonally gather in large colonies.

Northumberland and South-east Scotland

Essential Information

Locations and cliff walks: Alnmouth, Craster, Bamburgh, Lindisfarne; St Abbs Head to Cockburnspath (10 miles)

Distances from main towns: Berwick-upon-Tweed 12 miles; Newcastle upon Tyne 35 miles

Access routes: B1339/B1340 between Alnmouth and Bamburgh; A1/A1107 between Eyemouth and Cockburnspath

BR stations: Alnmouth, Berwick-upon-Tween, Dunbar

Youth hostels: Rock Hall, Wooler

OS maps: 67, 75, 81

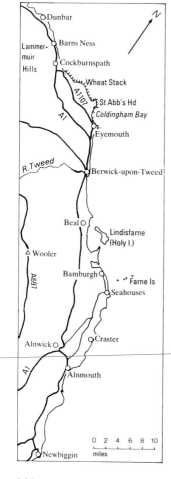

Northumberland

Dominated by the Cheviot Hills inland, the Northumberland coastline is something of a scenic anti-climax for lovers of high cliff coasts, especially when compared to neighbouring North Yorkshire. While it is craggy in places certainly, with one or two Whin Sill outcrops around Newbiggin, Bamburgh, and elsewhere, this long sea coast is more renowned for its fine sandy beaches, hauntingly imposing castles, and legendary off-shore islands.

For lengthier cliff footpaths, not indented with pockets of industry or holiday caravan parks, it is necessary to cross the Border and make for Coldingham Bay, north of Berwick-upon-Tweed. For those driving leisurely to Scotland, the minor-road alternatives to the A1 (M) are both restful and revealing. North of Alnmouth there are numerous access lanes to the shoreline contoured with sand-dunes and crags, together with quiet delights like Craster and the sea-edge walk to the fourteenth-century Dunstanburgh Castle, perched on an outcrop of the Great Whin Sill.

From Seahouses harbour, further up the coast, ferries ply to the Farne Islands, while from tiny Beal just to the north, there is a 3-mile causeway road open at low tide. The impressive seventh-century monastery ruins are an eloquent relic of early Christianity. It is, however, Bamburgh Castle that is the biggest draw hereabouts, a massive bastion on its rocky bluff. The village itself was the home of the lifeboat heroine, Grace Darling.

The Souter Stack, near Eyemouth.

Berwickshire

A pleasing introduction to the Scottish cliffs awaits almost immediately north of the Border. Around Coldingham Bay opposite the little resort of Eyemouth, St Abb's Head rises invitingly and heralds a superb line of headlands and inlets around Wheat Stack and Siccar Point, which culminates at Cockburnspath, perhaps familiar to walkers exploring the Lammermuir Hills.

Barns Ness, some 5 miles north, is a favoured touring base for naturalists, while just to the west of Dunbar is a cliff-top nature trail with splendid views across the Tyne Estuary towards North Berwick. This ancient burgh and pleasant resort, popular with golfers, lies just off the mainstream tourist track. Four miles away is craggy Gullane Bay, providing one of the best cliff walks in Lothian Region for walkers keen on bird-watching. There are still some remnants of Second World War fortifications, and even more damage through natural erosion, but nothing detracts from the wild beauty of the foreshore, or the distant views over the great Firth of Forth from the way-marked path along foreshore and cliff.

Climbing Information

The E. coast is ill favoured with climbable sea-cliffs. A few climbs have been made on stacks and walls of **dolomite limestone** at **Marsden** near South Shields. Further N. there are concentrations of climbs at:

● **Cullernose Point** (262 187): 5½ m. NE. of Alnwick; very steep cliffs of the Whin Sill formation – **quartz dolerite** – outcrop into the sea. This rock is columnary structured and provides a series of hard climbs, up to 80 ft high, usually up crack-lines or chimneys.

● **Castle Point** (260 220): 2 m. further N. beneath Dunstanburgh Castle. Here the Whin Sill overlies a layer of **sandstone** and the climbs encompass both rocks.

N. of the Border, the 4 m. of NE.-facing coast between **St Abb's Head** (913 692) and **Fast Castle Head**, in places up to 400 ft high, is composed of severely folded **dolerite** and **shales**, forming zawns, skerries, stacks, and other features. Some quite long climbs have been developed along this coast, the most concentrated at:

● **Fast Castle** (861 711): 7 m. NW. of Eyemouth. A convex, slab-like **dolerite** crag immediately below the castle ruins holds a variety of climbs of easier and medium grades, up to 200 ft. Over ½ m. E. stand The Souter Stack (120 ft) and The Brander feature, with climbs and shorter rock-problems.

Solway Firth and South-west Scotland

Essential Information

Locations and cliff walks: Dumfries, Kippford, Gatehouse of Fleet, Portpatrick, Mull of Galloway, Culzean
Distances from main towns: Dumfries 7 miles; Stranraer 6 miles; Ayr 8 miles
Suggested bases: Dalbeattie, Portpatrick, Ayr
Access routes: A710 between Dumfries and Dalbeattie; A75 between Gatehouse of Fleet and Stranraer; A715/A716 between Glenluce and Drummore; A719 between Turnberry and Ayr
BR stations: Dumfries, Stranraer, Ayr
Youth hostels: Mochrum, Ayr
OS map: 70, 76, 82, 83, 84

Solway Firth

The motorist who turns north and then west from Carlisle will discover a largely bypassed stretch of Scottish coastline, often overlooked by those hurrying to the Highlands. Long a favoured area for naturalists, the Solway Firth is rich in bird life; there is one of the largest and most interesting nature reserves in Britain at Caerlaverock south of Dumfries where the Nith empties into the Solway.

Although there are relatively few cliffs along the Solway coast, some stretches are craggy enough, lushly wooded between sandy bays for the most part, uncrowded and renowned for its spectacular sunsets. Kippford is a charming small-boat haven facing a vast sweep of the Firth which all but dries out at low water to become the feeding grounds of countless gulls and waders. Dalbeattie is a good base, with walking through nearby Dalbeattie Forest, and quaint hamlets like Palnackie to explore.

Further west, Gatehouse of Fleet boasts a spacious touring site in a scenic setting with good amenities including pony-trekking stables. Rocky outcrops and sandy bays abound and there is a worthwhile hill walk just inland towards Creetown, above the wide inlet of Wigtown Bay.

For the adventurous walker seeking coastal solitude, the Mull of Galloway is a worthy objective. South of Stranraer, itself a picturesque port and town of character, lies Gaelic Scotland, not unlike that to be found in the far north of the country. Tiny Portpatrick is delightfully located, surrounded by impressive cliffs, with fine walks beyond the ruins of Dunskey Castle. At the very tip of the dramatic rock headland of Mull stands a lonely lighthouse and some of the wildest cliff paths in Britain.

The south-west coast

Above isolated Ailsa Craig, at the southern end of the Firth of Clyde, Culzean Castle stands vigil on the Ayrshire coast. Now part of a Country Park, the setting is on a prominent cliff-top, surrounded by 600 acres of superb landscaped

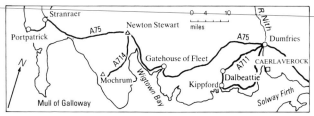

The Mull of Galloway.

and natural terrain. The castle is a Robert Adams masterpiece, one of the most popular in Scotland and now protected by the National Trust. There is some good cliff walking around both Culzean Bay and the Heads of Ayr.

Ayr itself is a bracing resort. It has a much-developed new town, yet with strong Burns connections and a history which goes back to the thirteenth-century. There are many delightful excursions for those who are prepared to walk, not least along the nature trails in the vicinity of the world-famous Brig o'Doon.

Climbing Information

Some rock-climbing has been developed on the **Rhins of Galloway**, largely on **granitic** and **porphyrite** intrusions on the W. coast and around the **Mull** (157 302).

North Scottish Coast

Essential Information

Locations and cliff walks: Lochinver, Durness, Tongue, Dunnet Bay, Duncansby Head

Distances from main towns: Thurso 5 miles; Wick 15 miles; Ullapool 25 miles

Suggested bases: Lochinver, Tongue, Thurso

Access routes: A835/A837 between Ullapool and Lochinver; A894 between Kylesku and Laxford Bridge; A838/A836 between Laxford Bridge and John o'Groats

BR station: Thurso

Youth hostels: Achmelvich, Durness, Tongue, Canisbay

OS maps: 9, 10, 11, 12

The road to Cape Wrath

Above Ullapool, where tourist traffic thins dramatically, the western seaboard and most of the hinterland looks more Scandinavian than Scottish. Mountainous at first, then declining to lower hills further north, stern verging on hostile. It is an area of countless lochs and peat bogs, traversed by single-track roads often higher (and drier) than the surroundings. It is 50 miles from Ullapool to Cape Wrath as the crow flies, a further 70 miles eastwards to John o'Groats.

Lochinver is a base for the adventurous and experienced hill-walker or climber, attracted to the challenging Sutherland hills; it is also favoured by anglers. The Youth Hostel at Achmelvich is located on a wild headland overlooking The Minch; from here a minor coast road winds tortuously above Eddrachillis Bay to the ferry of Kylesku.

Around the coast the terrain is so splintered it is difficult to define where the land and sea meet, especially towards the remote crofting hamlet of Scourie. Cape Wrath can be reached by ferry across the Kyle of Durness and there is a seasonal mini-bus service available for those who want to visit the most north-westerly lighthouse on the British mainland. The sea-cliffs here are spectacularly rugged, the area one of the most populated in the British Isles – by gannets.

Durness to Tongue

Dramatic limestone cliffs and cave complexes lie near the village of Durness, where there are usually more sheep than people, while a winding coast

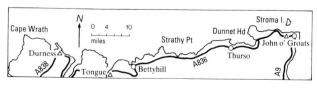

Left: Am Buachaille ('The Shepherd').
Above: Stacks near Lybster.

road traces the shoreline of Loch Eriboll, then bridges the Kyle of Tongue. The old loch-side road here has become popular with walkers and cyclists. Bettyhill is another angler's mecca, while the head-land of Strathy Point with its many caves carries one of the last lighthouses to be built in Britain (completed 1958).

Thurso to Duncansby Head

A slightly gentler coast, and easier road, lead east through Thurso. Near by, Dunnet Bay boasts one of the most beautiful silver-sand beaches in Europe, with the majestic Dunnet Head forming the northernmost tip of Britain's mainland – not John o'Groats, as popularly held.

It is a coastline of infinite beauty, with views across Pent-land Firth to the towering crags of Orkney. John o'Groats, like Land's End, has its share of tourist notoriety, but is not yet over-commercialized. There are lofty cliffs between Gills Bay and Duncansby Head, with the Island of Stroma lying just offshore.

Climbing Information

While there are several large sea-cliffs around the NW. coasts of Scotland, and while the NE. coasts are almost continuously cliff-girt, there has been little serious climbing development. Notable is the **Cleit Dubh** (322 728), 4 m. E. of Cape Wrath, a huge wall of **Torridonian sandstone** and the highest mainland sea-cliff in the kingdom. There are, however, many fine sea-stacks, two of which have become famous and quite popular climbing expeditions:

● **Am Buachaille** (201 652): 7 m. S. of Cape Wrath. Great obelisk of **Torridonian sandstone**, 200 ft high, gives a fine climb at HVS. Tidal.

● **Old Man of Stoer** (016 353): 9 m. NW. of Lochinver; attractive arrow-headed pinnacle, approachable only by swimming, gives a superb 230-ft climb on **Torridonian sandstone**.

Islands

A total of something like a thousand islands dot the seas around Great Britain. Of these, the majority are miniscule, it is true, but even so there are more than enough of sizeable variety to suit the most avid of walkers and climbers. Climbers in particular have long been attracted by the wilder cliff faces that are to be found offshore of the mainland, especially around the north of Scotland. Walkers have roamed the islands from the gentle Wight to wild Skye, while since the upsurge of backpacking, pedestrian explorers have been probing the more distant island groups in increasing numbers.

Air-ferry services now operate widely, bringing even the most far-flung islands within relatively easy reach. The ferry boats still carry the vast majority of summer visitors; for foot-passengers these little ships provide cheap and simple access to parts of the British Isles which are often quite unlike any mainland scene, as well as some that have

1 Isle of Wight
2 Anglesey
3 Island of Skye
4 Island of Arran
5 Inner Hebrides: Mull
6 Inner Hebrides: Islay and Jura
7 Outer Hebrides: Lewis and Harris
8 Orkney
9 .Shetland

remained virtually unchanged for centuries.

At one extreme, the Isle of Wight, now neatly tamed and much urbanized, with its heavy influx of summer visitors, is best walked outside the high season. In spring or autumn the walker can still hope for solitude. At the other end of the scale, it comes close to true adventure to board the ferry-boat bound for Lerwick, in the Shetlands. This island is 110 miles distant from the Scottish mainland, 12 hours sailing into the North Atlantic from Aberdeen. Here Gaelic is more often heard than English and the islanders have perhaps a greater affinity with Scandinavia than Britain.

Island exploration becomes addictive, especially with those people whose workaday life is bound by urban constraints. The contrast is total; the therapeutic reward of striding the wilder sea-girt landscapes, undeniable.

Practical Points

● In summer, Scottish car-ferries are very busy. Prior booking is advisable for any distant destination, though the short route to Skye, across the Kyle of Lochalsh, operates frequently and at all hours during the holiday season. The Isle of Wight route between Portsmouth and Fishbourne is so popular that it is almost obligatory to reserve space during July and August.

● Islands are invariably windy places, the outermost ones often gale-torn. Be prepared with top-quality waterproofs and rather more warm clothing than would normally be needed for mainland walking. Keep away from cliff edges, however tempting. Wind gusts of sudden and powerful force are common across high, west-facing headlands.

● Sometimes small on the map, it is surprising how lengthy island coastlines can be, particularly for walkers. Orkney main island – Mainland – for instance, has 200 miles of tarmac road, twice this mileage and more around the deeply indented shoreline. Do not set over-optimistic mileage targets.

● Do not climb island sea-cliffs on impulse. Tidal rise and fall is often immense around the northern Scottish isles. Beaches can quickly become immersed. No matter how alluring or secluded a beach may appear, think about the dangers of becoming marooned or worse, before scrambling down.

● Stay on recognized footpaths at all times on more remote isles and do not stray too far from havens unless with a party or local guide. Even on well-visited Skye, people have become lost for days among the more desolate and uninhabited Cuillin Hills.

● If circumnavigation is irresistible, pick an island that provides practical staging-posts. Wight, Anglesey, and Arran are good examples. Offshore objectives like these are well endowed with coastal roads and frequent pockets of civilization.

Isle of Wight

Essential Information

Area: 23 miles long; 13 miles wide

Car-ferry routes: Portsmouth–Fishbourne; Southampton–Cowes; Lymington–Yarmouth

Sea-cliff locations: Bembridge to Sandown; Ventnor; St Catherine's Point to The Needles

Distances from main towns: Ryde 5 miles; Newport 7 miles

Suggested bases: Bembridge, Ventnor, Totland

Access routes: A3055 between Brading and Freshwater

BR stations: Ryde, Brading, Sandown, Shanklin

Youth hostels: Totland Bay, Yarmouth, Wooton Bridge, Sandown, Whitwell, Shorwell.

OS map: 196

The southern half of the island – England's largest – provides the best walking, notably between Culver Cliff and The Needles. The island Tourist Board ensures that walkers enjoy the fullest access to beauty areas with a full range of descriptive leaflets available from the Newport office. Linked together, the selection of way-marked trails encircle the island, providing a 60-mile pedestrian route. There are seven separate long-distance paths in all.

The island is bisected from east to west by a chalk ridge; the southern coast is formed of a succession of splendid cliffs, themselves incised with deep ravines, or chines. The most famous is Blackgang Chine,

beyond St Catherine's Down, intriguing if heavily commercialized. There is much crowding here and elsewhere on the island during the summer months, which is why leisure walking is most favoured in spring or autumn.

Around Bembridge on the eastern side the landscape is still largely rural, a terrain of fertile undulations backing a cliff headland. The path traces a route around Foreland and lofty Culver Cliff. It declines to beach walking on approach to the holiday strip between Sandown and Shanklin 5 miles distant.

Ventnor to The Needles

Ventnor is the resort with the prettiest location, seawards of the 770-foot St Boniface Down and spilling down the chalk cliff in terraces. Here, The Undercliff (a geological landslip like that near Lyme Regis) was created when a chalk layer separated from the underlying sandstone. This luxuriant and deeply wooded shelf extends from Dunnose to St Catherine's Point, backed by cliffs.

There is fine open walking from here above four scenic bays – Chale, Brighstone, Compton, and Freshwater. The coast path (Tennyson Trail) culminates at the western end of the island with Alum Bay; the cliff strata form a vertical pattern of bright hues. At the furthest tip of the island are The Needles, so familiar yet of surprising impact when seen at close quarters. The distance from St Catherine's Point to The Needles is 15 miles.

Above: The Needles from Alum Bay.
Below: Alum Bay.

Anglesey

Essential Information

Area: 21 miles long; 19 miles wide
Hill and sea-cliff locations: Holyhead Mountain, South Stack, Bull Bay and Carmel Head
Suggested bases: Holyhead, Amlwch
Access routes: Ferry Bangor to Beaumaris (summer only), or via A5 Menai Bridge to Holyhead; west of A5025 between Valley and Amlwch
BR station: Holyhead
Youth hostel: Bangor, mainland side of Menai Strait
OS map: 114

The landscape of Anglesey is gently undulating with much treeless hinterland that is scenically dull. The A5 trunk road that cuts across the island for 20 miles to Holyhead reveals little of interest from Menai Bridge westwards. Only at the crossroads of Valley does the prospect brighten, revealing why 80 square miles have been designated as of outstanding natural beauty, notably on Holy Island to the west, and around the extreme northern coastline.

Anglesey is littered with many prehistoric relics – burial chambers, stone circles, cairns – and in places still bears reminders that this was once a Druidic society. As with many islands, it is the coastline (strongly reminiscent of the West Country in parts) that provides the real attraction, especially for the leisure walker. There are three particularly attractive and striking stretches along the 124-mile-long coastline.

Holy Island

The first, Holy Island, is itself an entity, 8 miles long and nearly 4 miles wide, linked to Anglesey by two causeways. It was an important landing place for early Irish Christians. Holyhead Mountain (720 feet) is the highest point, its craggy bulk looming steeply above Holyhead town and harbour. Various paths lead up on to the mountain from Holyhead, but it is most easily climbed from the western side. From the summit, crowned by an Iron Age fort, there are wide views, extending over the Snowdon range and even as far as Ireland. On the south-western side stands South Stack lighthouse, accessible via the chain bridge and 380 steps cut into the side of the mountain; visitors are welcome at certain times of the year. There is some exhilarating walking between North and South Stack islets, around Gogarth Bay, but beware the

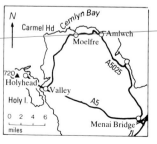

Left: South Stack, near Holyhead.
Above: From Castell Helen, Holy
Island.

climbers' paths to the bottoms
of the awesome cliffs which are
dead ends.

The Anglesey coast

Anglesey itself offers the
walker a very attractive stretch
of coast between Carmel Head
and Amlwch on the northern
seaboard, especially in the
vicinity of Cemlyn Bay and
Cemaes Bay (now National
Trust reserves), and also towards Bull Bay, where the reef
of The Mouse lies just offshore
of the rugged cliffs.

There is another line of cliffs
worthy of exploration from
Moelfre to Lligwy Bay on the
north-eastern coast. This headland is dramatic not only for its
natural grandeur, but also
because it is the graveyard of
many ships. The wreck of the
Hindlea, which went down in
1959, can still be seen beneath
the water near the Lifeboat
Station. Ynys Moelfre, the islet
just offshore, is a wildlife
preserve.

Climbing Information

Rock-climbing is concentrated at
the NW. corner of Holy Island
below Holyhead Mountain on a
series of large, dramatic, and
daunting cliffs above Gogarth Bay.
The rock is **quartzite**. All climbs are
in the higher grades, VS–XS and
typically vertical, strenuous and
serious. The exception is on Holyhead Mountain itself (see below).
Most climbs, but not all, rise from
deep water and are reached by
traverses or abseil. These cliffs are
perhaps the 'forcing ground' of
high-standard British rock-climbing
and claim international repute.

● **Craig Gogarth + North Stack**
(216 835): some 2 m. NW. of
Holyhead town; holds well over
100 climbs, up to 380 ft in height
besides several long girdles. Cliffs
are virtually continuous for ½ m.
and face W.

● **South Stack/Castell Helen** area
(206 820): 2 m. W. of Holyhead;
some 50 climbs, the longest 420 ft,
and several traverses, on dramatically twisted and folded rock – a
much more indented coastline –
facing SW.

● **Holyhead Mountain** (219 825):
holds a series of small crags on its
SW. flank, 1½ m. W. of Holyhead,
with a quantity of less steep short
climbs, up to around 120 ft, many in
the easier grades.

Island of Skye

Essential Information

Area: 50 miles long; 23 miles at broadest
Car-ferry routes: Kyle of Lochalsh–Kyleakin; Mallaig–Armadale (seasonal)
Mountain and sea-cliff locations: Black Cuillin, Red Cuillin, Trotternish Escarpment, Duirinish SW. Coast, Minginish SW. Coast, Trotternish E. Coast
Suggested bases: Portree, Dunvegan, Glenbrittle
Access routes: A850, Kyleakin to Portree via Sligachan; A863, Sligachan to Dunvegan via Carbost; minor road from Carbost to Glen Brittle
Youth hostels: Broadford, Glenbrittle, Uig, Raasay
OS maps: 23, 32

Skye is the jewel of the Hebrides. A complex island, indented by no less than fifteen great sea-lochs, it forms a knot of jutting peninsulas: no part of the island is more than 5 miles from the sea. The jagged coastline extends over 900 miles. Despite being a popular stop on the tourist trail, Skye remains a unique and tranquil island, suffused with two thousand years of Gaelic culture which still governs the pace and way of life today.

Most walkers and climbers are drawn irresistibly, sooner or later, to the unique Cuillin mountains. They are the most dramatic in Britain. Less well known, however, are the other fine mountain ranges and spectacular coasts. These, together with the typically fickle weather – sun, rain, and mist – and the romance of Bonnie Prince Charlie, combine to invest Skye with its magic.

The Black Cuillin

A serrated crest of black gabbro, gashed, pinnacled, and sometimes knife-edged, forms a 7-mile horseshoe round remote and wild Loch Coruisk. Typically these savage mountains are bare rock above the 1000-foot contour, hung with a succession of deep, crag-walled corries. Sgurr Alasdair (3309 feet) is the highest peak but there are some thirty other summits, none of them easy and most requiring scrambling or even rock-climbing to reach. The last summit was not climbed until 1898.

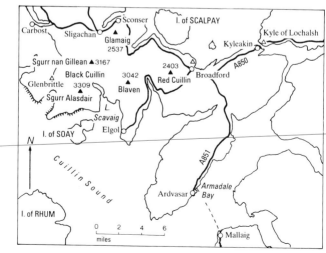

Black Cuillin: Sgurr nan Gillean.

Over: Loch Coruisk and Cuillin peaks.

The favourite centre for the Cuillin is Glenbrittle, a small sea-side settlement with a camp-site, a climbing hut (B.M.C.), and some accommodation. A difficult walk of some 7 miles between the mountains and the sea leads to Coruisk and the stunningly beautiful white sands, skerries, and clear green waters of Loch Scavaig into which it drains. The Loch can also be reached from the village of Elgol – one of the finest viewpoints of the Cuillin – by a strenuous walk round the coast via the deserted bay of Camasunary below the outlying peak of Blaven (3042 feet). Just before reaching Scavaig, one must cross the famous 'bad step' – a few feet of scrambling up an easy slab above the sea – it is really no problem. This must be one of the most dramatic walks in the kingdom. It is worth noting that after heavy rain both these approaches may involve dangerous river crossings.

The Red Cuillin

Sligachan, little more than an inn at the A850/A863 road junction north of the Black Cuillin, is dominated by the striking Black Cuillin peaks of Sgurr nan Gillean (3167 feet) and Am Basteir – 'The Executioner'. A rough path traverses deep Glen Sligachan for 8 miles south to Camasunary, at first beneath the distinctive and shapely scree-covered mountains of the Red Cuillin range. Highest is Glamaig (2537 feet), easily ascended from Sconser in little over two hours. After 4 miles, beneath the red peak of Marsco (2414 feet) – an excellent

157

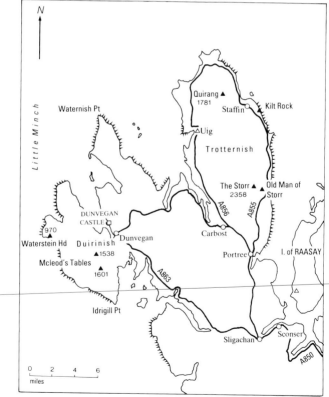

viewpoint – a faint track leads off south-west to cross the Druim Hain ridge to Coruisk. This is the easiest approach to the heart of the Black Cuillin. But the compass is unreliable on Skye and it may be difficult to follow this route in mist.

Trotternish

Northward stretches the long Trotternish peninsula with the pretty Braes region, looking across the Narrows to interesting Raasay Island, at its base. Raasay is reached by ferry from Sconser. Seven miles north from Portree, with its picturesque harbour, rears The Storr, at 2358 feet the highest point of the bizarre Trotternish Escarpment. Five hundred-foot basalt walls fall eastwards towards the coast road while grassy slopes sink west. The escarpment continues for 19 miles and can only be crossed in a few places. Beneath the Storr cliffs, among other peculiar towers stands a striking 160-foot cigar-shaped pinnacle, the Old Man of Storr. South of Staffin, the sea-cliffs are especially fine and include the famous Kilt Rock composed of vertical basalt pillars.

The Quirang, at the escarpment's northern end, is a geological oddity, a secret area of greensward, high among the basalt cliffs, encircled by weird rock towers. It was once used to hide rustled cattle and is best reached by a mile of cliff-bottom path from the summit of the Staffin – Uig road.

Duirinish

The south-west coast of this peninsula, accessible from the ancient McLeod stronghold of Dunvegan Castle, holds the most magnificent sea-cliffs on Skye. The cliffs stretch for over 9 miles along a deserted coast from Waterstein Head, towering 970 feet sheer above the sea, to Idrigill Point, above the three imposing 200-foot stacks of McLeod's Maidens. Inland the hills rise to the twin mesas of 'Mcleod's Tables' – Healaval Mhor (1538 feet) and Healaval Bheag (1601 feet) – the latter providing a wonderful panorama, south-east to the Cuillin, westward across the Little Minch to the long line of the Outer Isles.

Climbing Information

A veritable paradise for climbers, the exceedingly rough **gabbro** of the Black Cuillin provides rock-climbs of all standards, a large proportion of them in the middle and easy grades. The special delight is the superb scrambling, and the traverse of the crest line of many a corrie is an entertaining excursion for the competent climber. Classic traverses are:

● **Main Ridge**: the complete traverse, end to end, of the Cuillin. Over 7 m., several climbing pitches up to D and some 10 000 ft of ascent and descent. Fair time, 10 hrs, Garsbheinn (468 187) to Sgurr nan Gillean (472 253) but has been completed in 4 hrs 9 minutes.

● **Dubh Ridge**: 3000 ft, starts from shore of Loch Coruisk (479 205) and links the 3 Dubh peaks by their E. and W. ridges. A steep pitch on Sgurr Dubh Beag is usually abseiled. Finish on Sgurr Dubh na Da Bheinn (455 205), 3069 ft.

The largest single concentration of rock-climbs in the Cuillin is in:

● **Coire Lagan** above Glen Brittle and below the N. and W. faces of Sgurr Alasdair (449 208). More than 100 climbs, up to 1000 ft in length (all grades). Many on the huge cliff of **Sron na Ciche** (444 205): ½ m. long and 1000 ft high, famous for the great Cioch pinnacle rising from the cliff face at half-height.

159

Island of Arran

Essential Information

Area: 20 miles long; 11 miles wide
Car-ferry routes: Ardrossan to Brodick; Claonaig (Kintyre) to Lochranza (seasonal)
Mountain and sea-cliff locations: Mountains lie in two groups in N. half of island, main group highest point Goat Fell NE. (2866ft), lesser group round Beinn Bharrain in NW. (2368 ft); sea-cliffs: Cock of Arran, Holy Island
Access routes: Off A841 coast road; B880 between Brodick and Blackwaterfoot
Youth hostels: Lochranza, Whiting Bay
OS map: 69

Arran is becoming increasingly popular as a holiday island in the Firth of Clyde, almost a Scottish Isle of Wight, although less crowded in summer and more leisurely in pace and atmosphere. Brodick is the principal town and port, nestling in a sheltered bay on the eastern side of the island. It boasts a new Information Centre, useful for those wishing to enquire about cycle hire or pony-trekking.

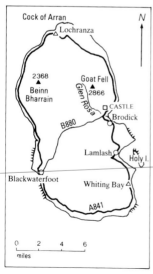

The island enjoys a climate mild enough for sub-tropical plants to flourish on the sheltered east coast where Brodick Castle and its beautiful gardens is a major attraction (National Trust for Scotland), and the prevailing westerly winds are partially blunted by the proximity of Kintyre to the west. Arran offers some of the best hill-walking in Britain, and walkers will appreciate especially the privilege of being able to roam, more or less at will, across mountains, moors, or coast. There are some 60 miles of coastline to explore, nearly all of it within easy reach of a road. A rugged stretch of coast surrounds the great sandstone bluff of the Cock of Arran, the island's northern tip, while deserted Holy Island, rising to 1030 feet and reached by boat (or swim) from Lamlash, is an exciting excursion.

Completely ringed by a coastal road, Arran is dotted with a wealth of non-intrusive tourist accommodation. A geologist's paradise, Arran is justifiably popular with naturalists also. The Red Deer population exceeds 2000 and amid the quieter glens, some strikingly beautiful, live rare species like the Golden Eagle and Peregrine Falcon.

The mountains

Most walkers will be attracted to Goat Fell (National Trust), a 3-mile ascent by a good path which starts through the grounds of Brodick Castle. From the 2866-foot summit an extraordinary panorama unfolds, encompassing the mainland coast, the Kyles of Bute, the great rock of Ailsa Craig, and, close at hand, a range of pinnacled peaks that radiate

On the summit of Beinn Tarsuinn.

from fang-like Cir Mhor (2618 feet) – certainly one of Britain's finest mountains.

All these sharp summits are ice-carved from a giant granite intrusion and cluster round the heads of two lovely glens, Sannox and Rosa, that penetrate the mountain complex from north and south respectively. The Rosa Water especially contains pretty waterfalls and delightful bathing pools. There are twelve summits of unique character and cyclopean architecture, but springy turf cloaks all but the rockiest slopes, and paths wind between the granite towers on all but the narrowest ridges.

These ridges give superb walking: the easiest links Cioch na h'Oighe (2168 feet), rising almost from the sea, to Goat Fell and is straightforward if airy. The best is the traverse from Beinn Nuis (2597 feet) to Suidhe Fhearghas (2018 feet) – only 5 miles on the map – via A'Chir, Cir Mhor, and Ceum na Caillich. This is a strenuous but classic full day's excursion and strong walkers should not be intimidated by the reputation of its only difficulties, the 'mauvais pas' on the exposed and narrow crest of A'Cir – a mile-long ridge, in itself the best scramble on the island – and the great cleft of the Witch's

Step on Ceum na Caillich, both of which can be avoided at lower level if necessary.

There is good but easier walking among the north-western hills, easily ascended from Pirnmill, with views both of the main peaks and across the sound to Kintyre and the distant Paps of Jura.

Climbing Information

The small group of high mountains, only some 4 by 5 miles, holds no less than 7 major (and several minor) crags on which nearly 200 different rock-climbs have been recorded. Rock is a coarse-grained **granite** – usually sound with notable exceptions.

● **Cir Mhor South Face, Rosa Pinnacle** (965 429): 5 m. NW. of Brodick; a striking, prow-headed buttress, 1000 ft high, faces S. and dominates Fionn Coire at head of Glen Rosa. Some 40 climbs on this face, a few in the easier grades but mostly middle and upper standard.
*'South Ridge Direct': 1100 ft. VS (1941)
*'Sou'wester Slabs': 340 ft. VD (1944)

● **Beinn Tarsuinn, Meadow Face** (962 412): 4½ m. NW. of Brodick. A great arcing buttress rises nearly 1000 feet and faces SE. Nearly a dozen climbs (all grades).
*'The Rake': 530 ft. VS (1962)
*'Meadow Grooves': 320 ft. VD (1944)

Inner Hebrides: Mull

Essential Information

Area: 27 miles long; 30 miles wide
Car-ferry routes: Oban to Craignure; Oban to Tobermory; Lochaline to Fishnish
Mountain and sea-cliff locations: Benmore; Tobermory Bay; between Lochdon and Lochbuie
Suggested bases: Tobermory, Craignure, Dervaig
Access routes: A849 between Loch Scridain and Salen; A848 between Salen and Tobermory
Youth hostel: Tobermory
OS maps: 47, 48, 49

The Island of Mull, the third largest in the Hebrides, lies to the west of Oban, beyond the Firth of Lorn. Although sterner than Arran, more exposed, and with a high rainfall, Mull is none the less fascinating. The landscape consists largely of wet moorland, particularly in the north, although this is now increasingly being taken over

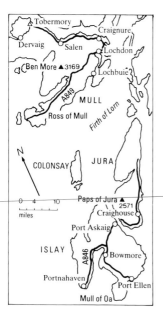

by vast plantations. The Forestry Commission administers 35 000 acres of terrain, and as a result facilities for visitors have been much improved in recent years. There is now a good choice of nature trails and way-marked walks.

There is great potential for hill-walkers. If not craggy, the mountains are extremely shapely. Ben More (3169 feet) is the highest point and the finest ascent is from Glen Clachaig by the interesting north-east ridge: but beware! The compass is unreliable here! An easier route is from the north-west. The high moorlands are characterized by 'traps' – terraces weathered in the basalt core of the hills. There is fine walking on the granite-tipped Ross of Mull with superb sandy bays and pink cliffs of up to 200 feet. Rudha na Uamh, the south-west tip of the Ardmeanach peninsula to the north, is interesting too: it holds several good caves, one of which, MacKinnon's, is reputed to be the largest in the Hebrides. Here too there are wonderful fossil trees and cliff waterfalls, but the going is rough.

It is, however, Tobermory Bay with its legend of Spanish gold that is the most romantic corner of the island, and also a mecca for small boats. The story that a fortune in ducats lies in the celebrated Armada wreck still exerts a draw. Those walking the forestry trails near Tobermory may ponder, before the glorious natural setting is seen as the real wealth. The walk to the ancient ruined castle of Aros, or to the headland lighthouse at the eastern end of Bloody Bay, reveals the true treasure.

Inner Hebrides: Islay and Jura

Essential Information

Area: Islay: 25 miles long; 20 miles wide. Jura: 28 miles long; 8 miles wide

Car-ferry routes: Whitehouse (Kintyre) to Port Askaig (Islay)

Mountain and sea-cliff locations: Islay: coast between Port Ellen and Claggain Bay; Bowmore to Laggan Point. Jura: Paps of Jura; coastline south of Craighouse

Suggested bases: Islay: Bowmore, Port Ellen. Jura: Craighouse

Access routes: Islay: A846 between Port Askaig and Port Ellen; continues as a single-track road with passing places along eastern shoreline of Jura

OS maps: 60, 61

Sgurr Dearg (2429 feet).

Separated by the mile-wide Sound of Islay, the two islands of Islay and Jura lie west of Kintyre. Islay, south-west of Jura, is more fertile and prettier. Jura, by comparison, is largely peat bog, uninhabited save for one small area around Craighouse in the south-east corner.

The most visited districts of Islay are Bowmore, where there is interesting rocky coast walking to Laggan Point at the mouth of Loch Indaal which bites deep into the island centre; and along the coast around Port Ellen. Between here and Ardtalla to the north-east, where the road ends, is a dramatic stretch of beautiful bays, offshore islets, and woods. There are fine views of Kintyre. The western side of the island is more fertile, although with much peat-covered terrain. The rocky coast between Portnahaven and Kilchoman is accessible by minor roads and is almost as wild and remote as that of Jura.

Jura, where George Orwell wrote *Animal Farm*, is a stern, barren landscape. The only road runs along the southern and eastern coastline, but the western coast is geologically interesting with its classic 'raised beaches' and more caves and natural arches than any other coast in the country. The three Paps of Jura dominate the southern half, rising to 2571 feet on the summit of Beinn an Oin: they are bare, scree-covered mountains, best admired from a distance. Those who do trudge to the summits are rewarded by views which extend, on a clear day, from the Isle of Man to Ireland. For the adventurous walker, the track from the roadhead at Ardlussa passes Orwell's farmhouse and reaches, after some 10 miles, An Cruachan, the far northern tip of the island, above the famous Gulf of Corrievrecken with its notorious whirlpool.

Climbing Information

Islay

The island's highest cliffs fall from the southern tip of the Oa peninsula, and the broken 350-ft **granite** cliff below the **Mull of Oa** (270 414), 5½ m. SW. of Port Ellen, offers good scrambling.

Climbs have been made on the fine cliffs extending some 1½ m. E. to **Beinn Mhor**, where interesting granite aretes fall some 650 ft to the sea.

Outer Hebrides: Lewis and Harris

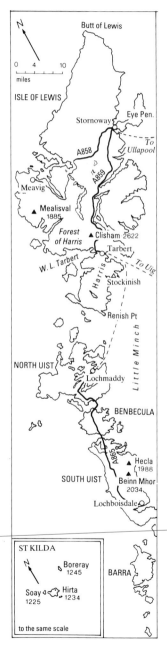

Essential Information

Area: 62 miles long; 30 miles wide
Car-ferry routes: Ullapool to Stornoway (Lewis); Uig (Skye) to Tarbert (Harris)
Mountain and sea-cliff locations: Lewis: Stornoway Bay, Loch Roag. Harris: Tarbert and south-east coast, Forest of Harris
Suggested bases: Stornoway, Tarbert
Access routes: A858 Stornoway to Loch Roag; A859 Renish Point to Loch Seaforth
Youth hostel: Stockinish (Harris)
OS map: 8, 13, 14, 18

The Isles of Lewis and Harris are in reality an entity, one land-mass separated by Loch Resort and Loch Seaforth. The landscape of Lewis is typically more Finnish than Scottish, more water than land in the centre, a vast peat moor and scattered, remote crofts with scarcely any high ground. Yet it is an atmospheric place, its translucent light as yet unpolluted, despite the growth of Stornoway, the largest port and town in the Western Isles.

Lewis does have some fine craggy hills in the west, south of Uig. Mealisval (1885 feet), steep and rocky, is the highest and gives wide views to the Flannan Isles and St Kilda. Uig itself, its rugged coast indented with beautiful bays of white sand, is delightful. The coastline of the Eye Peninsula and East Loch Roag, on East and West coasts, is also attractive.

North Harris, however, is dominated by a chain of interesting mountains rising above wild glens, and carved from that oldest of rocks – Lewisian gneiss – and granite. Five peaks top 2000 feet, the highest being Clisham (2622 feet): its narrow summit is reached most easily from the southeast. The road along the north shore of West Loch Tarbert gives easy access to the other peaks. This is popular country for walkers, climbers, and anglers.

Ferries and causeways lead to North Uist, Benbecula, and South Uist. On this last island the shapely peaks of Beinn Mhor (2034 feet) and nearby Hecla (1988 feet) rise steeply above a remote east coast. The traverse of the two summits is an interesting expedition. There are fine dunes and sands along the west coast.

St Kilda

This fabulous archipelago, 52 miles west of the Outer Hebrides, is a series of sharp rocky mountain-tops rising from the sea. For those lucky enough to reach them, there is exciting walking, scrambling, and bird-watching: visitors are certain to be captivated by these tiny and most remote islands of Britain. The last inhabitants, dependent on a seabird economy and thus natural rock-climbers, left in 1930 and the largest island, Hirta, is now reoccupied by a small military garrison.

Largest of the four main islands is Hirta, some 2 miles by 2 miles and rising to 1397 feet on Conachair. Awesome precipices fall northward from this summit, the highest sea-cliffs in Britain.

Standing off steep little Boreray (1245 feet; 1 mile by 1/2 mile), the second island some 4 miles north-east of Hirta, are Britain's two highest sea-stacks, Stac an Armin (627 feet) and Stac Lee (544 feet): both were climbed by the natives to harvest the gannets who nest on these fantastic rock pillars in vast numbers. Visiting climbers have since ascended both and discovered that, once a hazardous landing has been effected, Stac an Armin is straightforward but the ascent of Stac Lee is a very difficult and serious climb.

While the rock of the islands is granite, gabbro, and basalt, climbers have generally been disappointed, finding possible routes either too intimidating and dangerous or merely scrambling. They have, however, never regretted their visit!

Climbing Information

Lewis

Exposures of foliated **granite** among the hills of Uig. Several cliffs have been climbed on, including:

● **Tamanaisval**: 1530 ft (043 238) 6½ m. S. of Uig; a steep and impressive NE. face rises some 600 ft.

● **Teinnasval**: 1625 ft (041 254) 5½ m. S. of Uig; climbs up to 450 ft on W. face.

● **Griomaval**: 1625 ft. (012 221) 8 m. SW. of Uig; climbs on the 800-ft N. face.

Harris

Several fairly large and some smaller cliffs. Rock is **gneiss**. One cliff has seen much development:

● **Strone Ulladale** (080 136): 9½ m. NW. of Tarbert. This truly awesome cliff rises 1200 ft and holds Britain's largest overhang. Well over a dozen climbs of between 400 and 900 ft (several in easier grades). The overhang itself gives a desperate aid climb. In all, nearly a mile of cliff facing N., NE., and W.

● **Sgurr Scaladale** (163 084): 5 m. N. of Tarbert. Several climbs have been made on this large NE. face up to 800 ft in length.

South Uist

Beinn Mhor – Coire Hellisdale (810 323): 8 m. N. of Lochboisdale. Over a dozen climbs have been made here on steep **gneiss** and up to 800 ft. Cliff faces NE.

Orkney

Essential Information

Area: Mainland: 17 miles long; 23 miles wide. Hoy: 13 miles long; 6 miles wide
Car-ferry route: Scrabster to Stromness (Orkney Mainland)
Hill and sea-cliff locations: North-west Hoy; west coasts of Mainland and Hoy
Access routes: Mainland: A965 west of Kirkwall; off B9056 north of Stromness. Hoy: minor roads south from B9047 at Linksness
Youth hostels: Kirkwall, Stromness, Hoy
OS maps: 5, 6, 7

Green and fertile Orkney Mainland is low-lying, mild of climate, but ferociously wind-blown at times; it holds the sunshine record for the British Isles. Farmed more than fished, the landscape is notable for its neat crofts, wildlife (especially seals), wealth of prehistoric relics, and all-pervading atmosphere of Norse and Celtic past. Kirkwall, the capital, has a bustling, attractive harbour, some very ancient buildings, and even a fine cathedral. The A965 road west

is dotted with neolithic sites and chambers. At Maes Howe, 9 miles from Kirkwall, is the most impressive chambered tomb in Europe.

Though never really high, the western coast of Mainland is almost entirely cliff-edged: rough pasture or undulating moorland approaches the cliff-tops. There is much splendid coastal scenery and several superb sea-stacks. Notable areas are Marwick Head, where the cliffs fall sheer for nearly 280 feet, crowned by a memorial to those who were drowned, including Lord Kitchener, when H.M.S. *Hampshire* was mined in 1916; and the area round Yesnaby further south. between them is the Bay of Skaill, one of the prettiest in Orkney, noted for its bird haunts. Mainland is one of the finest sites in Britain for the study of seabirds, and has three reserves. A rich variety of species may be studied almost anywhere around the deeply indented coastline.

The southern islands encircle Scapa Flow, the once famous anchorage and virtually an inland sea. A ferry links Stromness to Linksness pier on Hoy, wildest of the islands. The population is around 250 and accommodation should be arranged beforehand through the Stromness tourist office.

Hoy is filled with empty heather-clad hills, in stark contrast to Mainland: it has been designated as of high scientific interest. Highest point is steep, rounded Ward Hill (1565 feet), and from its summit both Caithness and Fair Isle can be seen. Neighbouring Cuilags (1420 feet) falls sheer to the sea at St John's Head, the second

The Old Man of Hoy.

highest sea-cliff in Britain and culminating point of the stupendous cliffs which form Hoy's western coast. The only break in this 12-mile wall is the little bay of Rackwick, a deserted crofting settlement set in striking surroundings. A 2-mile walk northward above the cliffs, where great skuas breed among the heather and boulders, leads to the Old Man of Hoy – Britain's most celebrated sea-stack, 450 feet high.

Climbing Information

The cliffs are horizontally bedded **old red sandstone**. A fair amount of climbing has been done – but it is for experienced climbers only. The following are well known or important:

Mainland

Standard Rock (301 304): off Costa Head, 13 m. N. of Stromness; fine sea-stack, 220 ft S. (1970) approach by swim.

Yesnaby Castle (281 154): 4½ m. NW. of Stromness; fine sea-stack, 90 ft. HVS (1967) approach by swim.

North Gaulton Castle (216 134): 3½ m. NW. of Stromness; fine sea-stack, 110 ft. VS (1969) approachable by tyrolean traverse.

Island of Hoy

Old Man of Hoy (176 008): 2 m. NW. of Rackwick. Finest sea-stack in UK. 450 ft. Three different routes (all hard), easiest now popular. HVS (1966) approachable at all tides.

St John's Head (185 035): 1140 ft. Two different routes, 1969 and 1970. Latter climb XS, took 5 days' climbing.

Shetland

Essential Information

Area: Mainland: 56 miles long; 20 miles at widest point

Car-ferry route: Aberdeen to Lerwick (Mainland)

Hill and sea-cliff locations: Lerwick region, south-east coast, and St Ninian's Island; North cape, Stenness region

Suggested bases: Lerwick, Sandwick

Access routes: A970 Lerwick to Sumburgh Head (south); A970 and B9078 to Stenness (north)

OS maps: 1, 2, 3, 4

Shetland is the most far-flung of the British Isles, on the same latitude as Helsinki, and 110 miles offshore where the Atlantic and the North Sea meet. It has jumped from obscurity to prominence with the development of Sullom Voe, now one of Europe's largest oil ports. Yet those seeking the Norse and Celtic past, the most majestic of cliff scenery, or the richest variety of seabirds, can do so and scarcely be aware of this vast, carefully sited fuel complex.

There are over a hundred islands in the Shetlands group, only 14 of which are inhabited, with the majority of the population living on Mainland. The islands are of great geological variety, with large areas of sandstone and schists and much intrusive igneous rock as well, particularly in the west. The landscape is extensively peat-covered and virtually without trees, but in season the moors can be covered with wild lupins. The climate is mild but windy and gusts of 100 mph are not unknown.

In kindly summer weather, however, it is an island paradise for nature-lovers, bathed in that distinctive bright light for most of every twenty-four hours. Lerwick, the centre of 4000 years of turbulent history (itself surrounded by no less than sixty prehistoric sites), is the acknowledged base. It has a surprisingly busy harbour and town, with a fine museum of ancient treasures and a helpful tourist office.

On an island where one is never more than a couple of miles from the sea, there is particularly spectacular scenery south of Scalloway, where southern Mainland is at its most dramatic. The 12-mile walk via the Clift Hills to St Ninian's Isle (which is really a promontory) gives magnificent views extending over the offshore islands.

Interesting coastal scenery surrounds St Magnus Bay in north-west Mainland, where

the Ness of Hillswick displays especially fine cliffs of brilliant variegated colours and weird stacks, caves, and voes. Offshore rise the impressive pillars of The Drongs. North of Ronas Voe, with its red granite crags, rises Ronas Hill, at 1475 feet Shetland's highest. It can be

Unst: the coast (above) and fishing-boats on the beach (below).

easily gained from the A970 at Collafirth. From this height there is a sweeping panorama, and appropriate finale, across the geographical roof of Great Britain.

169

Useful Addresses

The Backpackers Club, 20 St Michael's Road, Tilehurst, Reading, Berkshire RG3 4RP

British Mountaineering Council, Crawford House, Precinct Centre, Booth Street East, Manchester M13 9RZ

The Camping Club of Great Britain & Ireland Ltd, 11 Grosvenor Place, London SW1 0EY; Northern England Office (Association of Cycle and Lightweight Campers), 22 Holmsley Field Lane, Oulton, Leeds

The Caravan Club, East Grinstead House, East Grinstead, West Sussex RH19 1UA

The Countryside Commission, John Dower House, Crescent Place, Cheltenham, Gloucestershire GL50 3RA

The Countryside Commission for Scotland, Battleby, Redgorton, Perth, Tayside PH1 3EW

The Forestry Commission, 231 Corstophine Road, Edinburgh EH12 7AT

The Ordnance Survey Department, Romsey Road, Maybush, Southampton SO9 4DH

The Ramblers' Association, 1–5 Wandsworth Road, London SW8 2LJ

The Scottish Youth Hostels Association, 7 Glebe Crescent, Stirling FK8 2JA

The Youth Hostels Association, Trevelyan House, 8 St Stephen's Hill, St Albans, Hertfordshire AL1 2DY

Further Reading

R. Adshead and D. Booth, **Backpacking in Britain**, Oxford Press

T. Brown and R. Hunter, **Spur Book of Map and Compass**, Spurbooks

R. Clark and E.C. Pyatt, **Mountaineering in Britain**, Phoenix

A. Clarke and I. Price, **Start Rock Climbing**, Stanley Paul & Co.

J. Cleare and R. Collomb, **Sea Cliff Climbing in Britain**, Constable

J. Hillaby, **Journey through Britain**, Granada

M. Marriott, **The Footpaths of Britain**, Queen Anne Press

M. Marriott, **Mountains and Hills of Britain**, Collins Willow

M. Marriott, **Start Backpacking**, Stanley Paul & Co.

D.G. Moir, **Scottish Hill Tracks**, John Bartholomew

W.A. Poucher, **The Lakeland Peaks**, Constable

W.A. Poucher, **The Welsh Peaks**, Constable

W.A. Poucher, **The Scottish Peaks**, Constable

W.A. Poucher, **The Peak & Pennines**, Constable

W.A. Poucher, **The Magic of Skye**, Constable

R. Aitken, **The West Highland Way**, Her Majesty's Stationery Office

J.H. Barrett, **The Pembrokeshire Coast Path**, Her Majesty's Stationery Office

A. Falconer, **The Cleveland Way**, Her Majesty's Stationery Office

B. Jackman, **The Dorset Coast Path**, Her Majesty's Stationery Office

S. Jennett, **The Ridgeway Path**, Her Majesty's Stationery Office

S. Jennett, **The South Downs Way**, Her Majesty's Stationery Office

J.B. Jones, **Offa's Dyke Path,** Her Majesty's Stationery Office

B. Le Mesurier, **The South Devon Coast Path**, Her Majesty's Stationery Office

F. Noble, **The Shell Book of Offa's Dyke Path**, Queen Anne Press

E.C. Pyatt, **The Cornwall Coast Path**, Her Majesty's Stationery Office

T. Stephenson, **The Pennine Way,** Her Majesty's Stationery Office

A. Wainwright, **The Pennine Way Companion**, Westmorland Gazette, Kendal

C.J. Wright, **The Pilgrims Way and North Downs Way**, Constable

Index

Page numbers in italics refer to illustrations.

INDEX

INDEX

Acknowledgements

British Tourist Authority: 19, 59, 61 (below)
J. Allan Cash: 24, 53, 61 (above), 63, 66, 67, 80, 85, 118, 143 (both), 147, 153 (below), 154, 169 (both), jacket
John Cleare Mountain Camera: title-page, 17, 21, 23, 27, 29, 31, 32, 33, 35, 36, 37, 39, 45, 47, 51, 69 (both), 71, 73, 75, 79, 82, 87, 88, 89, 90, 93, 95, 97, 99, 101, 102 (both), 105, 107, 108, 111, 112, 117, 121, 124, 127, 129, 134, 139, 141, 145, 148, 149, 153 (above), 155, 157, 158, 161, 163, 167
Wales Tourist Board: 135